OVER S!ZE

THE MEGA ART & INSTALLATIONS

Edited & Published by
Viction:ary

FOREWORD
—
BY KURT PERSCHKE

What does it mean to work in public space? We see art, architecture and design exploring the public realm in new ways. Conversations that once were about size are now about scale. Scalability as a concept bounces between the digital and material realms. Scalability in public space means moving from the older model of static mass toward public imagination.

As an artist working around the world, I see scale and public space through a particular lens. Playing with the urban landscape, my work changes scale in each site yet is always the same size. I am engaged in how public perception is shifted through this mercurial experience of scale.

For me the idea of 'public space' no longer connotes just designated communal zones. The construct of 'inside = private' and 'outside = public' is irrelevant today. It's no longer enough to plant monuments and assume they will enter into public discourse. To truly work in public now means to engage public imagination — for an idea to move into the public consciousness.

I am often asked what RedBall Project is about. Like much effective work in architecture and design, there is a slight of hand at play in this project. While standing in front of RedBall talking about the other sites it has visited, taking a picture with a friend, wondering how it got there and where it might go, or where one would put it next, a person will ask me "What is it for?" And I think, "It's for you - right now." That moment of imagining, playing, questioning, considering — that is the work. When a person thinks, "I know where it should go next!" they have — perhaps without realising it — taken on my role as an artist. By implicating individuals in the act of creativity, the work moves beyond the physical moment into public imagination.

Our world moves toward greater complexity, spreading continuously outward yet often channelled through a phone. Scale remains a relative phenomenon. The language of sculpture is all the more relevant today with its elemental pull of physical presence, tactility, mass, material, form and, of course, scale.

PREFACE

Size intrigues when it appears atypical of the usual towards whichever ends. The greater the distinction, the stronger the magnetism, forcing us to hold our eyes on to that something to assimilate the particulars, make sense of it and have it lodged in our minds. The idea of size, or more precisely scale, is a sensation subject to space and our immediate awareness of our body. The phenomenon applies to all, from living things to artefacts.

The drawing power of size does not only allure spectators but also contemporary sculptors and artists, as both a challenge and a platform to play with ideas and forms. Taking size and scale to the extreme is not new in today's visual culture, evident in architecture, sculpture and photography. It is not only a result from technology improvements, but also artists' urge for breakthroughs, the growing potency of the media and the freedom that allows artists to endow media and forms with their own meanings by whim. Miniature figures dare artists to commit themselves to executing the finest and unimaginable details. Giant works, like architecture, challenge artists to articulate ideas through the planning and construction of space, ambiance and forms.

The domain of large works however seem to be prevalent in various parts of the world. For one thing, it goes without saying that monumental works are comparatively more visible, as they take up more physical space, which sometimes only city streets or into big galleries or museums can accommodate. Its ability to make a bold statement with great impact is another. In a world flooded with spectacles, the guarantee for visibility is in great demand. Everybody wants to be seen, known and remembered. For artists, people are the destination of a conversation. Without them, their work is incomplete. For galleries, companies, malls and cities, visitors bring business opportunities and spend.

Things that once can be held with one hand and perceived with a static gaze now require viewers to walk in order to apprehend the work to the full. Size functions in many ways before it captivates eyes. Most basic of all, again, is how it enables a work to be shared by a bigger crowd within the same space, at the same time. By summoning people to gather in the physical space for a palpable experience, some artists take it to invite viewers to re-approach their surroundings anew, like Florentijn Hofman's *Stor Gul Kanin* (p.076); Mehmet Ali Uysal's *Skin II* (p.177). Sometimes, for maximum impact, size is a response to space, see *Q-Confucius No.2* by Zhang Huan (p.020), or a tool to create an isolated atmosphere for event comers as in *Y150 NIssan Pavilion* by TORAFU ARCHITECTS (p.130). On another level, size enables double-reading as in *Waste Landscape* by Elise Morin and Clémence Eliard (p.042), which questioned the relations between materials (individually identified as discarded CDs) and its form (a shimmering landscape as a whole).

In two chapters, featuring in-depth interviews with selected practices and profiles of 39 artists currently working in this international vein, *OVERS!ZE* investigates how scale can be played up by means of quantity, driven by space, as well as the artists' intention to communicate and engage.

Starting with conversations with 12 artists who have recently accomplished some of the most globally-known art projects, INTERVIEW delves into the creative process of a mix of self-initiated projects and commercial installations from the onset to see how they recognise size as an effective language and solution to arrest the public. Of them, German foursome, Inges Idee (p.008), Canadian sculptor Max Streicher (p.054), British artist Luke Egan, alias Filthy Luker (p.090) and Dutch artist, Florentijn Hofman have been dedicated to giant sculptures and art projects on a regular basis for a long time. Where intermedia artist Karina Smigla-Bobinski (p.030) extolled the vision of Ada Lovelace and Jean Tinguely with an interactive "machine", Gerry Judah (p.116) explains how size fits for celebrating the glorious history of names like Jaguar and Audi at the annual British Goodwood Festival of Speed since 1999.

In the second half of the book, GALLERY features 27 profiles, including artists like Urs Fisher and Seward Johnson; designers, such as Monstrum, Jean Julien; and advertising agencies, Mother London, who take pleasure in constructing a Brobdingnagian world in a bewildering array of forms, encompassing guerrilla art and street installations which we cannot settle for less.

INTERVIEW

For now or for good, for tour or for fixed display, the make of monumental installations is a long, challenging but rewarding process. This section reveals what happened along the way, from site visits to what follows the events, through the words of 12 artists and collectives.

Founded in Berlin in 1992, Inges Idee is a group of four individual German artists, who live and work in Berlin (DE), Cologne (DE) and Malmö (SE) respectively but join up to create whenever public art commissions come knock on their doors. Composed of Hans Hemmert (b.1960), Axel Lieber (b.1960), Thomas A. Schmidt (b.1960) and Georg Zey (b.1962), the collective recognises public spaces as the sum and substance of history, time and architects' works of art. Through site-specific sculptures, Inges Idee re-connects viewers to their surroundings with subtle hints, stretched forms and a sense of humour.

INTERVIEW
WITH

INGES IDEE

What do you build in general?

We build sculptures for the public space. We try to create open and poetic images, of which the sense and implication can be completed by the viewer himself. We invite the viewers' mind to be an important part of the artwork.

Most of your huge sculptures are custom-designed commissions. Where did the ideas come from?

Our ideas come from site-visits, speaking with the people involved, stakeholders and from researching the context of the site; on the other hand the ideas are always a mix of our individual pools of artistic ideas. For *Running Track* (2010), the intensely coloured sculpture combines the concrete, graphic aesthetic of sports, such as the lines of a racetrack, the sole of a sports shoe and the stripes of sports clothing, with the sculptural power of a dynamically curved form. The slight bend in the sculpture increases the potential of movement and at the same time places it in dialogue with the oval course of the road's drop-off loop. With its vital and moving expression, it refers directly to the activities on the site. The striking graphic quality of the lines and the exaggerated perspective give the work an explosive dynamic that is reminiscent of an animated cartoon. The laconic self-evidence and monumental size of the sculpture, however, creates a factual reality that cannot be overlooked and that puts an emblematic stamp on the area.

1 From Above, 2011
Expo 2005 Aichi Commemorative Park,
Global Center, Aichi (JP)
Fibre-reinforced plastic, steel
2.9 x 5.3 x 2 metres
Project management:
NANJO and ASSOCIATES
Photo: Kei Okano

2 Ghost / Unknown Mass, 2010
Towada Art Cente, Aomori (JP)
Fibre-reinforced plastic, steel
9 x 3.6 x 2.5 metres
Project management:
NANJO and ASSOCIATES
Photo: Sadao Hotta, Inges Idee

3 Running Track, 2010
Terwillegar Community Recreation
Centre, Edmonton (CA)
Fibreglass
4.4 x 7.6 x 2.5 metres
Photo: Raffaella Loro

4 Tall Girl, 2009
Orchard Central, Singapore (SG)
Fibre-reinforced plastic, steel
20 x 1 x 1.6 metres
Project management: Singapore Arts
Council, Kee Hong Low, Michelle Tan

5 Receiver, 2010
DR Byen, Copenhagen (DK)
Mirror-polished stainless steel
19 x 6 x 3.5 metres
Photo: Erling Jeppesen, Inges Idee

What do size and scale mean to your respective clients?

The clients want outstanding signpost and landmarks in city-landscapes based upon scale. For DR Byen, the new site of Danish Broadcasting Corporation in Copenhagen, Denmark, *Receiver* (2010) responded to the Danish radio's request for an expression of what the company does content-wise on the one hand, and an iconic sculpture which can double as a backdrop for broadcasting programs like daily news on the other hand. The piece was also expected to be able to cope with the highbrow architecture of Jean Nouvel's radio city hall next to the building. With its mirror-polished stainless steel, we built the sculpture which bundles its entire environment on the curved surface, as if it is a screen. The sky, the huge architectures and the passers-by. Factually and symbolically, it conveys a constantly timely reflection of the present-day world.

How do the proportions, size and scale of monumental sculptures matter to viewers? Do you think their significance varies with culture?

Everything is always related to the actual human size. The audience on the street is always impressed by monumental scale, like children are. They impress you because of the relation between large scale objects and the human body when it is, for example, a stretched human figure. For the idividuals who work mainly in galleries, it is impossible to work big because of the little money involved. But in public space the budgets are much higher which allow artists to think bigger. This phenomenon functions in all contexts and in all cultures.

Your sculptures make for a narrative response to its architectural environment. What kind of experience do you want to bring to the public audience?

What we want to do is to reach the viewer with his own individual experiences. We try to reach this by open, narrative stories; but these narratives always derive directly from the context of the site. To make this possible, we tell very simple stories of everyday life or Jacob Grimm's fairy tales, which everybody — even the children — in all cultures knows about. That way stories become clear and viewers would immediately understand the picture just by looking at the work without recourse to background knowledge. Because it is all straightforward, everyone can connect.

But they do not always come in the audience's sight directly, prompting people to survey their surroundings. Do the sculptures' meanings go away if the public fails to notice their existence?

Yes, we like to develop work which is not always obviously visible at first glance but the second. This would also ask for a higher everyday-awareness for the public audience if you want. Because in this modern society people tend to "switch off" their awareness of what is happening around as they are conditioned by the pictures in the media and advertising. We want to change this mode because we personally think it is important to live and be conscious of things and people around. Visitors can also ignore their presence, which is also part of the meaning for us as artists...

Distortion seems to be a recurring theme in your work as well. Why is it interesting to you?

Distortion and perspective deformation is a way for us to create works that look deceptively taller, and of course it plays with the parameters of looking. A child has to learn first the fact why something far away looks smaller and becomes bigger when you successively approach it. This is a crucial simple mechanism of looking at the world, like children see the world.

Some artists take on materials to convey meanings. Does it apply to your projects too?

We also convey meaning by using certain materials like bricks, wood or stainless steel, but on the other hand we as artists who mostly build outdoor are forced to be aware of the durability of the work, which are supposed to last for decades.

The members of Inges Idee live and work as individual artists in three different cities. How do the team work together?

Inges Idee is specified to work on defined projects in public space. We only react to invitations from clients. For such kind of projects we meet and try to find a good idea for the site. Inges Idee works as real "multiple authorship". We feel ourselves already so to say as a small "public-ness" which is able to discuss the context in a wider sense as we could do as individual artists. The three cities is bridged by phone, email, skype and... telepathy.

What are you planning on producing next?

We are producing for the moment a few new works for Canada and Germany. In Canada we are realising a giant ring of 20m in diametre functioning as streetlight on a highway-crossing near Calgary International Airport. In Germany we are building a 35-metre high electricity pylon for international exhibition, EMSCHERKUNST, near the city of Essen, which no longer stands stiff holding up the electric cables, but stands out and is starting to move and dance.

For the city of Bayreuth (DE) we realise a new monument for the romantic writer Jean Paul.

We hope to realise once the sculpture of a smart figure and let it strike out for his own thing while his head is up high 300m in the very clouds...

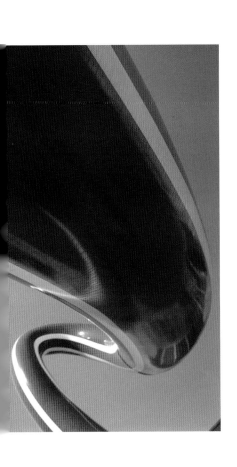

Born in Anyang, China, in 1965, Zhang Huan has made a name for his performances in the early 1990s after he finished his Master's degree in Beijing and moved to live and work in New York till 2005. Although Zhang has decided to return to China and settled in Shanghai since, his work continues to appear around the world, exploring spirituality and religion's role through materials and forms. Sitting at 66-metre tall with half of his body bathed in the floor, *Q-Confucius No.2* was one of the seven works Zhang has created site-specifically for his solo exhibition at Shanghai's Rockbund Art Museum. The silicon sculpture addressed global issues and posed a question at the religion situation in China today.

INTERVIEW
WITH

ZHANG HUAN STUDIO

What was *Q-Confucius No.2* about?

The Rockbund Art Museum invited me to do an exhibition in 2009. The staff of the museum were fond of my art-works and they showed great respect to my ideas. After serious discussions, the entire advisory board reached an agreement on the exhibition's theme, which was "Q-Confucius (Ask Confucius)", and through which we would express the general absence of religious and spiritual support among Chinese people amidst the ongoing, rapid social reforms today.

Shall we copy everything from the West or return to our traditions when human beings fail to remedy the damages they have caused, and the world is about to end as the price of what we did to the Earth? Or will there be a new set of spiritual values or religious beliefs on which we can rely? The project "Q-Confucius" highlights the great significance in both the present reality and the future.

Everything we know about Confucius is from text and drawings. What is your perception of him? What were you trying to portray through Q-Confucius?

Confucius was born in the kingdom of Lu in 551BC. According to the textual study, paintings of the sage dated back to Ming dynasty in ancient China. In 2011, I created Q-Confucius No.2, which consolidated its existence in history and in me as I revealed it. The details of Confucius' soul and flesh on display were the visualisation

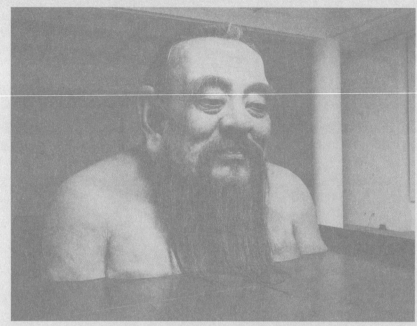

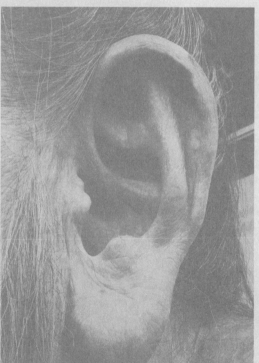

Q-Confucius No.2, 2011
Rockbund Art Museum, Shanghai (CN)
Silicone, steel, carbon fibre, acrylic paint
3.8 x 9.8 x 6.6 metres

of Confucianism — Confucius' philosophical and ethical systems that have been experienced and reinterpreted through various dynasties of China in the past and thus, been infiltrated into the history of Chinese civilisation.

In the process of making this sculpture, I spent a lot of time reviewing the master's philosophy. Among his thoughts and sayings I appreciate the sentence "At 70, I could follow whatever my heart desired without transgressing the law". There is wisdom behind the saying — a cultivated person does not fight against his fate. While things are on the contrary in the world of art, artists must transgress the general routine so as to achieve his goal.

I am always in pursuit of the sage's realm that at the age of 70, I would follow whatever my heart desired without transgressing the law.

There are many wise men in Chinese history. Why did you choose Confucius to address issues that the world is facing today?

While human beings are consuming too many resources on our planet, we are also losing our belief, resulting in today's spiritual crisis. People have no idea how to tackle their problems. Maybe the ideology of Confucius could offer a clue. The reason why I chose Confucius instead of Laozi or Zhuangzi was that the ideology of Confucius was pragmatic and also the most controversial.

How many versions of Confucius have you made in total? What do they represent individually?

Compared with my previous artworks in terms of materials and forms, the artwork of this exhibition is a significant breakthrough. In total, I have made seven artworks for the exhibition of "Q-Confucius", and among them four are distinctly different. In *Q-Confucius No.2*, recognising water as the source of life and everything in this world, I asked the audience to think again how we could cherish our world and resources by casting Confucius in silicon, gazing at his reflection in a shallow pool. As for a painting which illustrated Confucius teaching his disciples during a trip, I made my reverence by using ash for its special meaning to me. As well an unprecedented attempt in my creative approach, I also provoked alternative thinking by constructing a portrait of the sage with materials as unorthodox, austere and unique as cowhide; and interpreted the dual nature of man by situating a huge mechanic Confucius in a cage full of monkeys.

Q-Confucius No.2 is made true to life in every way but the size. How do size and scale matter in your work?

Size and scale don't matter to most of my work. What matters is the specific content that an artist wishes to express. For *Q-Confucius No.2*, size is merely a way to optimise the use of Rockbund's huge gallery space.

How would you say your sculptures have interacted with the environment, space and its audience?

I'd like to be in a free state when creating an artwork. And I hope the audience and critics can be in the same free state when they make comments on the works. All exhibited works (in the Confucius series) were specifically made according to the size of Rockbund Art Museum. The way of display was quite different from traditional and formal exhibitions inside museums. To integrate the collection with the neighbouring community, the works were shown both inside and outside the museum, i.e. an open exhibition space, to realise direct and mutual communication and interaction with the audience.

We perfectly integrated the works of art into the space, which would make people feel that the work was growing from the space instead of an artificial installation. I'd like to have new works for each exhibition. One of the most important features of contemporary art is to put forward questions. By means of this exhibition, we questioned and confronted what had happened and was happening around us. We hoped that the audience could also ask questions and have a deep thinking during their visit of the exhibition. After all, I have to be true to myself, as well as my work. I cannot just close my eyes and pretend I cannot see.

You've spent seven years in New York after you studied in China. What did you do in New York? How did your life in New York influenced your art?

I worked as a professional artist in the U.S. and did performance art all over the world.

People may be influenced by various life experiences and living environment. After several years of living abroad, I felt homesick and wanted to go back to my motherland, like the fallen leaves go back to the soil. The native culture and language supply me with more energy and nutrition for art creation.

The variety of material you've used to create is also key to your sculptural art. How many have you taken to create so far? Which of them is most interesting to use and why?

I am a person who likes to make changes. I always pursue something new. I don't like doing things repeatedly. I think concepts and languages really matter to art creation. Ash painting is my invention. To me, ash is not simply a medium for painting. It is the collective memory, collective soul and collective blessings of the people in China.

Where did *Q-Confucius No.2* go after the exhibition?

We are planning a tour.

What are you planning on producing next?

I was invited to have a solo exhibition in Palazzo Vecchio, the town hall of Florence. When it is realised, my artworks will be displayed inside the museum of Palazzo Vecchio and also in municipal plaza of Florence, in dialogues with the classical works created by great Renaissance geniuses.

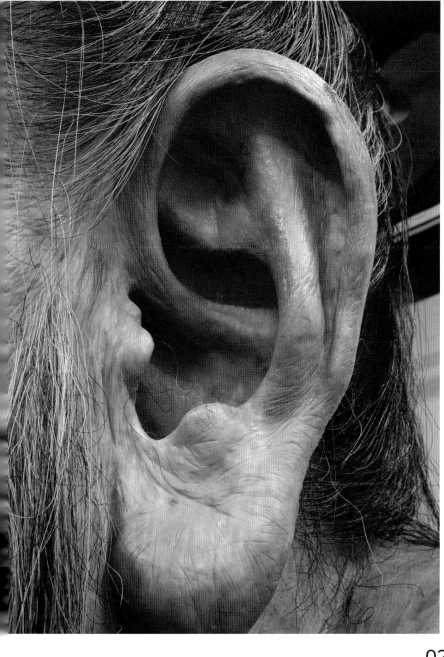

Splitting her life between Munich and Berlin, Karina Smigla-Bobinski explores interactive and mixed reality art between analogue and digital media. Her works encompass online projects, interventions and multimedia physical performances, as well as interactive installations like *ADA*. Built to draw within a space as a response to visitors' physical input, *ADA* extols Ada Lovelace and Jean Tinguely's visions of devising a machine that can produce art. Upon entering the exhibition space, visitors will soon find their ways to drive *ADA*, 'who' would in fact draw in 'her' own will.

INTERVIEW
WITH

KARINA SMIGLA-BOBINSKI

What was *ADA* originally produced for?

ADA is a result of my thoughts and inquiries about the fundamental idea of 'computer as a machine' that can remember and create works of art, such as poetry, music, or pictures like an artist. I have developed *ADA* without a client. After she was finished in 2010, curators Ricardo Barreto and Paula Perissinotto invited *ADA*, as the first, to FILE Festival 2011 in São Paulo, Brazil. Then came FAD Festival in Belo Horizonte (Brazil), FACT Foundation in Liverpool (U.K.), FILE Festival in Rio de Janeiro (Brazil) and ZERO1 Biennial in Silicon Valley (U.S.), etc..

What kind of influences do Ada Lovelace and Jean Tinguely have on you?

I am interested in the connection between art and science and, especially with *ADA*, the role of computers in our world today. Ada Lovelace was the first person who saw the potential generative power of a machine as Charles Babbage proposed Analytical Engine. That was just a vision — she saw a machine with the eyes of a poet, an artist.

I did the same by looking at "machines" today as an artist and building a post-industrial and post-digital "creature" that resembles a molecular hybrid (such as one from nano biotechnology) with the ability to produce artworks through an open source method. In connection to copyright debate, there appears a very interesting question too — what is exactly the work of art? The balloon, the drawings on the wall or both? :-)

On the other hand, Jean Tinguely was an artist who disapproved the commercialisation of art and had built kinetic artworks out of industrial age machine parts, of which some are generative, like Métamatics that could draw on its own. Some other of his artworks were designed to be self-destructive, which he described as "under destruction", a creative force and structural transformation. I developed the idea of Jean Tinguely, where a kinetic artwork expanded itself by the action with which I entrusted the visitors. The visitors thus became the driving force responsible for the expansion of *ADA*. From every aspect, Jean Tinguely paved the way for me.

With *ADA*, what kind of experience did you intend to bring to the public and the exhibition space?

The normal, traditional way of viewing art is to go to gallery and look, but the participation is confined to looking and nothing more. All reactions occur inside the viewers' head instead of physically to the piece.

Interactivity in art stands out as a way to connect with the audience. This contact between art and the public creates a relationship that involves the viewer personally in the project.

The best part of interactive art installations is when you can use your body which then turns you into a part of the art piece. When we talk about interactivity, we imagine it as a digitally-created, non-physical experience which computers and electronics have very often forced into the foreground. But *ADA* as a post-digital artwork does not need programming because *ADA* is an analogue interactive kinetic sculpture.

Same as my other works, it is very important for me that the entrance into the practical experience of art is possible for everyone and that visitors may decide how far they dip into the art experience according to their ability or will. I like the fact that visitors are able to work with the intuition in my installations and use their body to explain how they work. Here, as *ADA* is put in action by visitors, she would then fabricate a composition of lines and points which are incalculable in their intensity and expression. By exerting control on *ADA*, constantly visitors would fall into some kind of a trance as they try to govern *ADA*'s drawing path. Sometimes people forget where they are and that *ADA* is balloon vulnerable to damages. They might sometimes get a little bit too rough with her.

Do you consider *ADA* a machine or a being?

ADA is constructed to have her own will. Once you set her into motion she just works away. What *ADA* produces is very humane because she seems to respond to some of a human instincts. The only method to decode these signs and drawings is to understand them as the intuitive association of our jazzy dreams and thoughts.

It is a good feeling of having created a piece of art that is autonomous and that it would not be complete without visitors. Within the balloon-space-people relation, visitors are obliged to respond. That was my intention when I built *ADA* for the first time, but the reality got beyond my wildest dreams. Perhaps it is an intuitive reaction of the body that provokes us to stretch our hands to catch or push the ball and not let it drop. It floats weightlessly in the air and changes the perception. The more she is handled by visitors, the blacker she gets from the charcoal and thus seems more "alive". Even I, who built her, sometimes get the illusion that she is a living thing.

Already at her first public appearance in São Paulo, visitors asked where 'uma bola com carbon (a ball with charcoal)' was as they looked for *ADA*. But after they interacted with *ADA*, they referred to *ADA* using the name or "she", so did the many English visitors at FACT Liverpool. So it happened that I use "ADA" or "she" now, too.

Anyway the concept of *ADA* is a temporal "under destruction" artwork with her lifetime equal to the duration of an exhibition. Her age will progress with the number of people who visits her, their temperament and the galleries' supervision on site.

What was it like creating and building *ADA*? How did *ADA* conceive its unique form and look?

While Ada Lovelace's idea of a machine laid the grounds for *ADA*, in the new post-industrial age where the Web is born of a desire for speedy and open access to information and nanotechnology comes from a desire for speed and miniaturisation, *ADA* becomes the common ground for both nano-switch networks and human brains, which explains how she generates marks like when a switch-network configures itself to create "quick routes", in the structure of a synapse.

If, in this very serious scientific world, we could follow the White Rabbit and fall into the world of art, we might imagine that it makes no difference whether *ADA* is alive or not when we consider *ADA* as a nano creature. As Scottish physicist James Gimzewski concluded, together with Masakazu Aono, the creator of the first nano-switch, and Argentine neurologist Dante Chialvo, the basic mechanism of the brain is the same as the basic dynamics of nano-switches.

Knowing this and inspired by Ada Lovelace's poetic way of thinking, I took the idea of the nano-machine which then I manipulated on the scale against the standards with silicone, helium and carbon. I created an art machine, an independent creature capable of claiming the whole room for itself and eventually along with visitors.

How do size and scale matter to *ADA*?

Size and scale decide our perception and how we deal with the interactive artwork. The relation between our bodies and the artwork is crucial. If the artwork is smaller than we are, then it is subjected to us and thus, be absorbed or rejected. And if it is equivalent to our size, then it will mutate into a counterpart which we have to act toward. But when the artwork is bigger, much bigger than us, then it will become a superordinate which we are compelled to absorb and be subjected. We would have to respond to it, arrange ourselves or leave it.

For *ADA*, the last two conditions apply. Relatively equivalent in size, visitors would perceive ADA as their counterpart. As for the drawings which covered the entire gallery space, the lines would exert influences on the visitors, whom simultaneously become part of the work.

What do you expect the audience to take away after interacting with ADA? Is it necessary for them to understand why you built ADA?

In all exhibitions with *ADA*, I observed and spoke with the visitors (ranging from children to NASA employees). To those who reflected on this work, their ideas seemed to go with my thoughts. This is like a controlled free fall into the hole of the White Rabbit.

Similar, for example, to the experience of the still life paintings from the 17th and 18th century, the concern of a painter was on the one hand to grasp the nature and objects of everyday life in their beauty and play, and convey a hidden message or a mental content on the other hand. To read these coded messages (then as now) you have to dip deep into the art experience. However, those that remain on the surface, they also can find satisfaction in the aesthetics of visual experience (beauty of the presentation). There were also those who ignore all that and create his own reading mode and meaning. In this case, it was interesting for me to know their thoughts.

Where would ADA go after the exhibitions?

After the *ADA*s are back, they remain in the boxes in which they are returned to me. *ADA* is "under destruction", meaning they will not be washed or repaired. For a new exhibition, I build a new *ADA* and each *ADA* has only one life. I will rather continue to drive the destruction as I have in mind the decomposition of *ADA* into its individual parts and the parts might create small documentary sculptural objects as mementos of the interactions.

Among all the interactive projects you've been involved, which one do you enjoy most and why?

The first artwork that comes to mind is *ADA* because it is the current project, but also ALIAS which can be understood as a metaphor for the dependency of art — without a viewer or visitor it is trapped in an incomplete existence. The visitor are alienated in an intimate situation. The strange confrontation with the personal shadow and the appearance of a stranger inside creates a tension between individuality conceived within one's own silhouette and the presence of an image of somebody else.

What are you planning on producing next?

I am currently dealing with the phenomenon "cloud". More about that when it is ready.

ADA, 2010
FACT (UK), FILE Festival (BR), ZERO1
BIENNIAL (US), FAD Festival (BR)
Helium-filled balloon, charcoals
2.5 metres in diametre

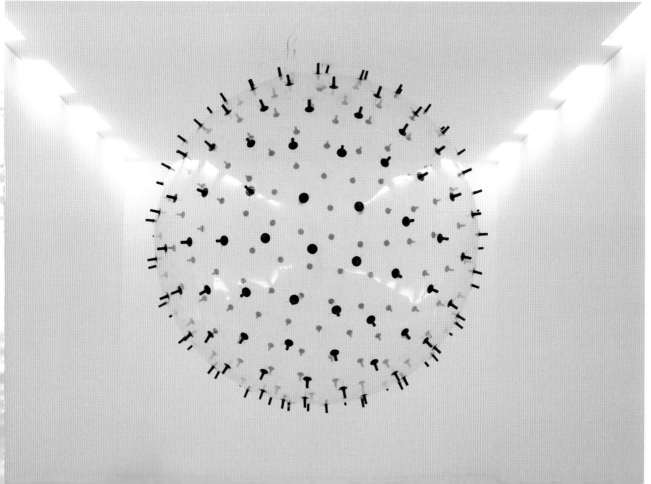

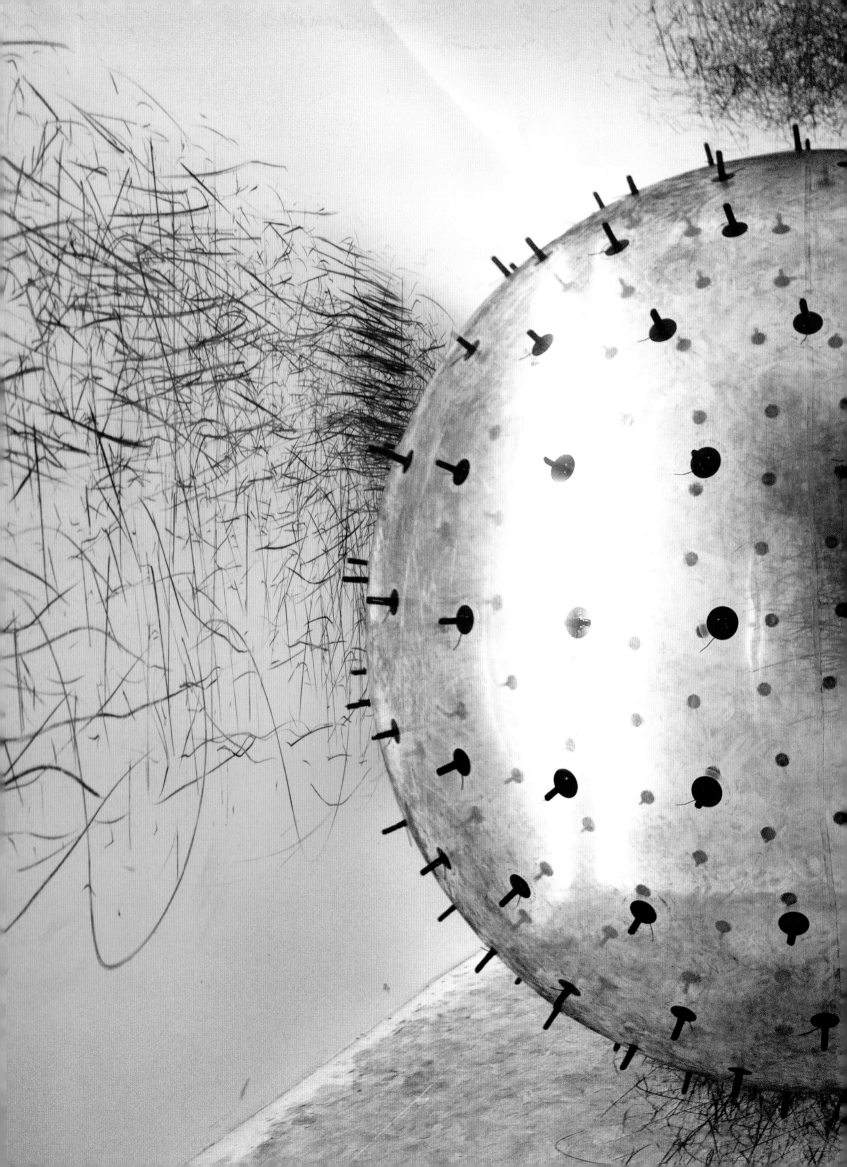

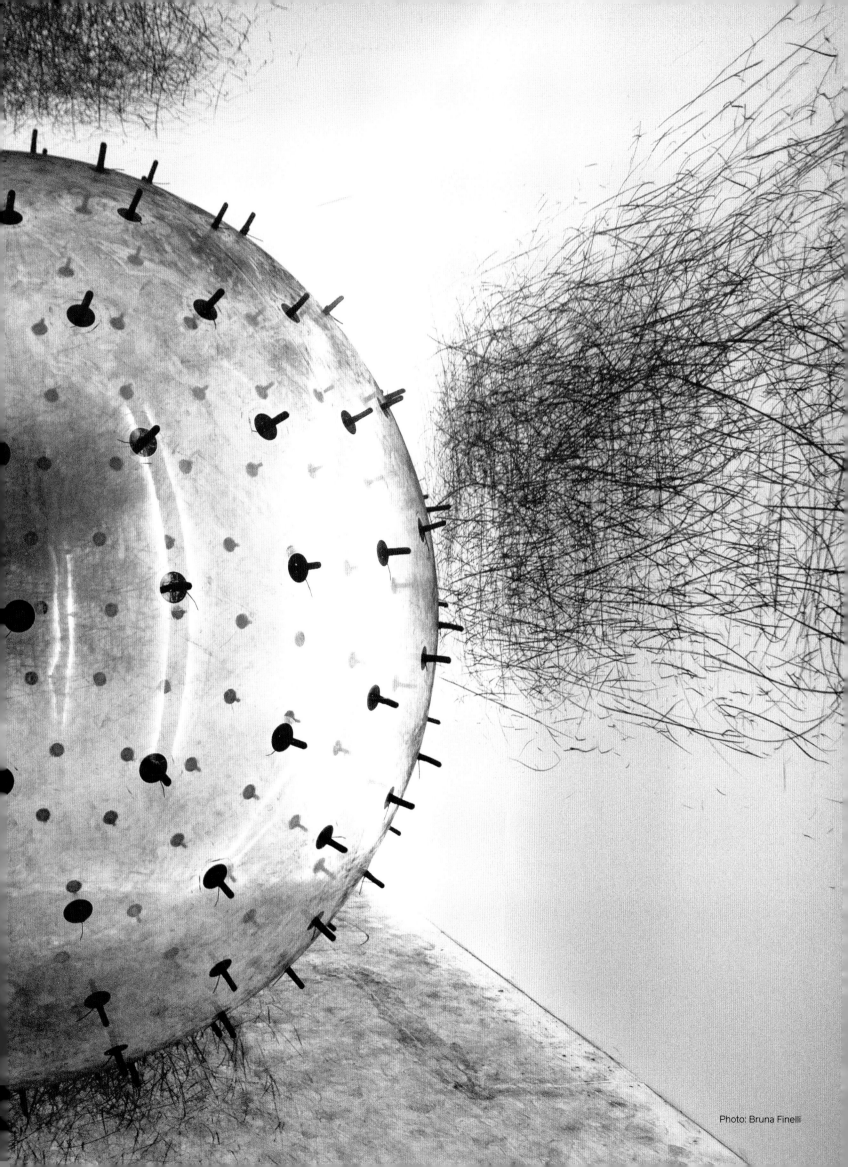

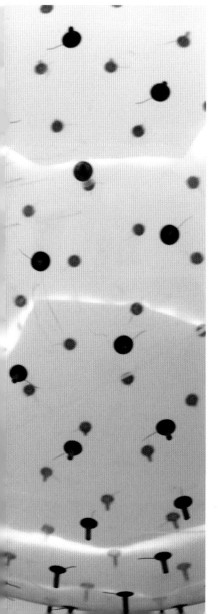

Elise Morin (b.1978) is a visual artist and Clémence Eliard (b.1976) is an architect. Living and working in Paris as individuals, the artists have cooperated since 2009. Ranging from video art to installations, Morin's work often seems to incorporate minimalism through direct reference with space or the repetition of unitary materials. Eliard now runs her office SML on architecture, design and artistic projects in Paris after her return from working in China. Using 65,000 discarded CDs hand-sewed together using wires, *Waste Landscape* criticised the economic displacement of objects and current environmental issues inside Centquarte, a former funeral home. The artificial landscape, the space and the discs told visitors of the migration of meanings as they united before visitors' eyes.

INTERVIEW WITH
CLÉMENCE ELIARD, ELISE MORIN

What was *Waste Landscape* produced for?

Waste Landscape is born of a desire to create an art installation of which the production process would be self-financing, and an infinite number of formal proposals. I (Elise) wanted a material that would allow a global project with which each step would be equally important. The installation itself is not the goal. The purpose was to build an installation that would be recycled.

What was the first thought that popped into your head when you were approached for the project?

My first thought when I pondered was how a possible representation of the contemporary landscape could be turned into a desert of plastic, a symbol of the vision of the Western society in the second part of the 20th century. In that way, the CD is a very symbolic creation of this vision of the economy and of this period. The planned obsolescence, short-term technology, entertainment and use of polycarbonate are married for better or for worse. The other issue is to represent an invisible landscape: the buried landscapes that are hidden or glamourised today, monumental waste disposal for example.

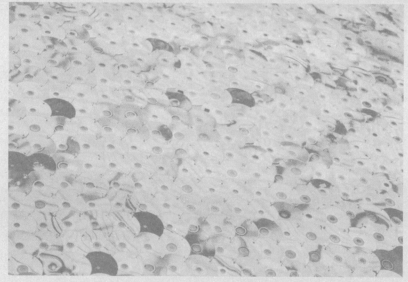

Waste Landscape, 2011
Le Centquatre, Paris (FR)
Unsold CD (65 000 pcs), wire, inflatable
(Floor space) 500 m²
Special credits: Alain Menuau,
Carole Cohen, Universal Music,
Sofricel, La Poste

Did you choose CDs as the core medium of expression? What kind of preliminary work was necessary before *Waste Landscape* started to take shape?

The weaving of CDs was a fundamental step for the design of the project. Each CD was pierced by three points and flakes with woven wire to assemble large homogeneous layers without damaging the material. This technique had helped preserve the polycarbonate forecast total recycling facility.

Inflatable domes were designed to measure. The idea of using the force of the wind as a mounting element allowed a great economy of materials and resources.

The CDs were intended to be recycled and return into the industry in the form of raw materials.

The project invited the public to walk around, explore and enjoy the landform like a real natural land-scape. What kind of experience did you intend to bring to the public during the event?

Double or triple reading was important to the project. I sought to create a fascination with the beauty of the poetic installation. While the first emotion, aesthetic contrast with the cynicism revealed the CDs as objects, the accumulation, weaving and traditional aspects of the production offered another door. It took a lot of time and patience to weave 65,000 CDs together by hand. I like the idea that a large audience can appreciate this proposition and the diversity of experience shows its richness — as a playground for children, a puzzle of economic, ecological and aesthetic issues, etc.. If the impact is purely aesthetic, it is not satisfactory. The installation should also be witness to its time, with critical but not necessarily negative visions to initiate discussions out of the sphere of contemporary art that also is rooted in the social and economic reality. It's a game between art, reality, the desire for a great read for the public.

How do size and scale matter to your project?

The scale is important to reinforce double reading. By far this is something near and it is nothing. The illusion of a massive, solid and precious landscape was lost when the unity and simplicity of the CDs was revealed. The metallic works only when the mass of CD is important.

As a sculpture or landscape, the multiplicity of viewpoints increases as the audience walks to examine the work progressively. Some see a boiling sea of mercury, others scales of a fish or reptile. Under the canopy of Le Cent-quatre, natural light gave its effect on the CDs as the sun or clouds. The installation is not always the same.

What was it like creating such an extensive installation? What were the things that required special attention during the process?

We did not have the resources to conduct a technical study, a prototype or a test. CD woven might not bear the strain of the domes. It could break at any time during the first inflation. Eventually the thousands of CD became an armour of scales and the dunes took shape. The bet was won on the day of the opening. The whole process was extremely intuitive.

The exhibition location was also key to the project's objective. How do you think art facilitate communication with the public?

The choice of locations must be consistent with the challenges of project. Le Centquatre is an art space housed in a former public morgue in Paris, in the 19th arrondissement. It is the desire to be in a public space, popular and access free. People could see the installation by accident on their way. During the few days before the show, we moved the work out of our production studio. Pedestrians were able to see the weaving in the hall and it has raised many questions, many exchanges and volunteers spontaneously joined the project. I really appreciated this experience. The appropriation of the concept by the public resulting from a simple choice of production has allowed the participation and support of the public. If the work is born in a Parisian workshop between Rue d'Aubervilliers and Rue Curial, the goal is to see it grow, develop and even turn to other cities. Her next exhibition will be held at TodaysArt Festival in the Hague, the Netherlands.

How was the collaboration on *Waste Landscape*? What brought you two together?

I am a visual artist and Clémence is an architect. I am very interested in architecture and Clémence is more drawn to poetry and art installations. We complement each other in our approaches. We share the same desire to offer poetic spaces and experiences. Architecture and art installations are mutually beneficial at many points. For example, we see the light with the same interest in our respective work, thinking in the design of a building to Clémence and for me, my artistic work. After *Waste Landscape*, we have also collaborated on another project entitled "nebula" exposed to Fontevraud Abbey in June 2012.

Where did *Waste Landscape* go after the event?

A new form of landscape, a new *Waste Landscape* was exhibited in The Hague on 22 September 2012.

If *Waste Landscape* is not travelling any more, the CDs will be recycled by a factory.

Are you planning on producing the likes of *Waste Landscape* in the near future?

"Water Carrier" is my new project. It features (seven) giant "meteorites" floating on a river spanning about 300 metres. Millers made of test tubes containing fluorescein of which the colour evolves with the weather. The exhibition took place at White Night, a sleepless night in Košice, Slovakia, on 06 October 2012.

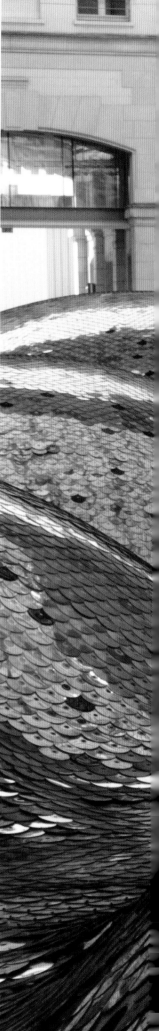

Having studied theology before his art education, Max Streicher's earlier work investigated contemporary spiritual values via comparatively natural-scale installations, image projections and text based on religious and mythological imagery. A shift in his creative focus occurred in 1989, where he mounted his first inflatable in a church, leading him to expand his techniques to deliver the unique sensory experience of air in kinetic sculptures and installations to exhibit with artist group, Nether Mind. Made to swell and contract using electronic fans, his inflatable sculptures put air on central stage, as the concrete indication of life and our existence.

INTERVIEW
WITH

MAX STREICHER

What do you make in general? What are you trying to explore through your works?

Inflatables have had an important place in my work since 1989. In most of these sculptures and installations I have used industrial fans and simple valve mechanisms to animate sewn forms with life-like gestures. Most of these works have been made of lightweight and papery fabrics such as Tyvek or nylon spinnaker. The weightlessness of these materials allows them to respond with surprising subtlety to the action of air within and around them.

Generally inflatables are an expression of naive optimism. In an art context they signal popular culture, anti-art and irony. I play with and against these expectations. The movement of air within my forms recalls our own sensation of breath — of breathlessness, of holding our breath, etc. My work exists in moments of kinaesthesia, when the movement of air within a form causes something to stir within the physical being of the viewer. This response is to more than just the obvious action of inflation and the robust occupation of space. What I feel is even more moving — the recognition of deflation, shrinking, vulnerability, silence and dying. My choice of extremely light and papery materials enhances this sense of absence and transience, of the nearly not there at all. Thus, the awakening occurs in our awareness of the tenuousness and fleeting nature of existence. My work with the inflatable medium is about moving the viewer from a playful and ironic headspace toward a physical connection to his or her most vital forces, physical and spiritual.

How did you get into building monumental sculptures?

My works gradually became monumental. The first large-scale work came about as the result of an open invitation. Gordon Hatt, curator of Cambridge Galleries, Ontario, offered me a large gallery and simply asked "what would you like to do?" I immediately envisioned a room full of giants. Later I was offered outdoor spaces such as rooftops and the works continued to become larger.

How does air function as a material in your work?

Breathing is the obvious function that my work focuses on. I use air to animate my works because it provides an effortless naturalism — it does not only look right, it feels right, recollecting our own sensation of breath. Breathing is first of all a matter of physical well-being, as we are dependent on the constant flow of air within ourselves, but breath is also intimately connected to our emotions, memory and spirit. The appearance of life-like movement within my works is often disrupted by actions that are distinctly unnatural. For example, a pair of figures that alternately inflate and deflate in a kind of life-giving/life-taking/life-saving dance as in *Blow* (2004) or *Romulus & Remus* (2005). While the sense that they are breathing makes them seem human or alive, it can also become macabre and preposterous when the absence of air reduces them to a thin and crumpled pile of fabric on the floor.

Breathe (1989), a two-metre high ram's horn, was my first inflatable that inflated by means of a found vacuum cleaner. *Breathe* was shown in a church. When viewers turned the vacuum on its loud roar would disrupt the peace and quiet of the church. The horn would fill and rise and then the vacuum would turn off and the horn would deflate. It was my lack of experience with making inflatables that really created this need to repeat the act of refilling air. Put simply, it leaked. But this was the beginning of many more works that would rise and fall, as if they were breathing. *Blow* was my first work in a professional context made after art school. It was a boisterous and irreverent reaction to the conceptual path I had been on in art school, meant to "blow off steam" and get back to some engagement with sculptural materials that I had somehow denied myself in a more conceptual photo-text-based practice. People described the inflation of the horn as "frisky" and it seemed fitting that such a creative, or generative action, such as an erection, should be in a place that worships the creator — the one who breathed life into dust.

What do size and scale project in your work?

In Latin, the word for air is the same as for spirit — Spiritus. I think the sense that my forms are breathing has a greater impact when it is experienced on a large scale. Viewers often report that as they move through the work, in particular the large breathing figures, they experience a sense of peace. Many have told me they want to curl up with the giants and sleep with them.

Their scale is embracing, potentially threatening, but the forms are also delicate and vulnerable. I think these various qualities are all about our ability, and desire, to connect to something other. The sense that something is breathing I feel engenders a kind of empathy, or as mentioned before a sense of kinesthesia, recollection of a physical memory. I'm told that by simply watching an athlete or dancer in performance we, the viewer, are rewarded with a hit of endorphins.

I think of spirituality as a process by which we connect with the other that brings us to a sense of wholeness. Looked at through this lens, art making, the creative process, the act of imagining and realising something that has never been, is a most serious and profound act of prayer.

Your giants are intended to overwhelm. What can shock bring to the public in public space?

My giants are meant to overwhelm, to make the viewer feel small and vulnerable, child-like perhaps. The function of shocking placement I feel is more evident in other works where unexpected placement, or displacement, are more a matter of context than of scale. Take *Endgame (Coulrophobia)* (2010) which consists of three clown heads stuck within an alley; *Stuck Unicorn* (2003), pushing its way out of the window of a Renaissance palace in Germany; horses rising out of a rooftop in *Quadriga* (2006); or clouds over a swimming pool as in *Alto Cumulus* (2006). Works like these reflect an interest in the metaphysical and recall the work of artists like Giorgio de Chirico or René Magritte with their placement of unexpected objects in rooms or public squares.

To what extent would you say your sculptures have interacted with the environment and space?

In many cases my ideas have occurred to me almost spontaneously when I've been shown a space, like the giants as already mentioned. Cloud occurred to me upon seeing the Tanenbaum sculpture court inside Art Gallery of Ontario. The divisions in the concrete floor and its reflective quality triggered a memory of flying over the southern Alberta prairies in a small aircraft. There were huge thunderheads all around and in such close proximity I felt like I was in a Tiepolo painting. This was the image I recreated. The architecture of the Hart House swimming pool pavilion has a neoclassical character which reminded me of the classical references in surrealist paintings. I was only aware later, when someone pointed it out to me, that in hanging clouds in this space I had created an homage to René Magritte.

What was it like creating and building installations that are so much bigger than you? Did you do all the tailoring and sewing with your own hands?

My studios have not been that large. Often I don't see the inflated work until it is installed. Working with inflatables has many advantages. One is that they can be created in close quarters. It all has to go through a sewing machine. Another is that they can be shipped easily. I have done most of the sewing myself. In recent years I have hired someone who mostly does the production sewing for editions of smaller works. She has also helped with handling some of the larger works that become heavy and too unwieldy for one person to move through a sewing machine.

What role do materials play in your art? Do you intentionally eschew colours in your projects?

I have preferred papery and neutral materials to the more traditional nylon used in commercial inflatables. My earliest works were all made of Tyvek, which is a synthetic non-woven, paper. I chose it, and later a similarly papery nylon spinnaker, as a way of distancing my work from commercial inflatable which are often in colourful nylon. I have used colour. My first clown head works were painted a puce flesh-like colour. Since then I have at time used recycled billboards. For example *Stuck Unicorn*, *Dung Beetle* (2005), *Floating Forest* (2011) and most recently, and most colourfully, *Vertical Constructions (Dancer #1 & #2)* (2012).

The off-putting, perhaps creepy, quality of *Dung Beetle* is enhanced by the material from which it has been constructed. In this case the shiny, black billboard material was chosen for its tactile qualities. It is very durable and stiff, carapace-like, and the printed surface has an insect-like sheen.

The use of this billboard material makes reference to the tradition of collage as a political tool for turning propaganda against itself. It is a satisfying experience to take this manipulative and authoritarian corporate materials which are then cut up and taken to reassemble to become something whimsical, generous and possibly terrifying.

Where do your sculptures go after the event?

Some of my works are in museum collections. Most are stored at my home and often continue to have an exhibition life, being adapted to new spaces.

What are you planning on or hoping to do next?

I am currently incorporating sound into my inflatables. In collaboration with sound sculptor, Garnet Willis, we have made our first playable inflatable pipe organ. It sounds just like a pipe organ but it's surprising for its configuration and strange shape. I revisited my *Floating Forest* for this first organ and we mounted pipes in the branches. It has been shown this autumn in Toronto in the first instance hanging, and in the second piled up like a "brush pile". Ideally it can be installed so that people can move within the arrangement and hear the pipes sounding from all around them.

1,3 Cloud, 2004
Art Gallery of Ontario, Toronto (CA)
Inflatable sculpture, tyvek, clear vinyl, electric fans
9.75 x 9.75 x 7.3 metres
Photos courtesy of Art Gallery of Ontario

2 Architecture of Cloud, 2010
Art Gallery of Hamilton, Ontario (CA)
Inflatable sculpture, tyvek, electric fans
Size varies
Photos courtesy of Art Gallery of Hamilton

4 Alto Cumulus, 2004
University of Toronto, Toronto (CA)
Inflatable sculpture, tyvek, electric fans
9.75 x 9.75 x 7.3 metres
Photo: Gordon Belray

5,6 Sleeping Giants (Silenus), 2002
Toronto (CA), Metz (FR)
Nylon spinnaker, electric fans
8 metres in height each

7 Floating Giants, 2001
Muzik Building, Toronto (CA)
Nylon spinnaker, helium-filled balloons
7 metres in height each

8 Quadriga II, 2007
Union Station, Toronto (CA)
Nylon spinnaker, electric fans
10.5 metres in height each
Photo: Tyson Williams

9 Quadriga, 2006
Ludwig Forum for Contemporary Art, Aachen (DE)
Vinyl, electric fans
6.5 metres in height

10 Stuck Unicorn, 2003
Kunsthalle Erfurt, Erfurt (DE)
Recycled billboard vinyl
5 x 9 x 2 metres
Photo courtesy of Kunsthalle Erfurt

11 Dung Beetle, 2005
Toronto (CA)
Recycled billboard vinyl, electric fans
9.2 x 6.4 x 6.1 metres

Photo: Falko Behr (top),
Luminous Productions (bottom)

11

Born in Delfzijl, the Netherlands, in 1977, Florentijn Hofman loves his work big. With his subjects acquired from everyday objects and materials unique to local culture, his site-specific sculptures get to viewers' heart as a positive, sensational artistic statement. One of his most popular piece is *Rubber Duck*, a conventional bath toy blown up into a 26-metre tall inflatable, having stopped off in 11 cities ranging from Auckland and São Paulo to Osaka. Although very often exhibits are fenced, visitors' presence, as well as the surrounding, is crucial to Hofman and his sculptures.

INTERVIEW WITH

STUDIO FLORENTIJN HOFMAN

What are your projects about? Your sculptures called up people's childhood fascinations. How are these sensations pertinent to the audience?

They express a change of perspective. Because (as) the objects get bigger, you would better say I make the world smaller.

We are emotionally bonded to our toys. In memory our toys often look bigger but as you grow bigger, objects become proportionally smaller. So maybe some of my work can take the audience back to a time where everything was less problematic and difficult and make them feel free again. By looking at my sculptures, you can let go all concepts of what you have been taught and what remain 'true' is that it's playtime again.

How do these toy animals relate to you and your audience?

You get these toy animals as well as plastic models made in Hong Kong or China at the dentist as a child if you done well. These objects relate to all in different ways, like how a painting, sculpture, music, theatre, etc. connect with its viewers.

1 Fat Monkey, 2010
Pixelshow, São Paulo (BR)
Flip flops (10,000 pcs), inflatable
5 x 4 x 15 metres

2 Rubber Duck, 2007-present
Sydney (AU), Osaka (JP), Auckland
(NZ), Hasselt (BE), etc.
Inflatable, pontoon, generator
max. 26 x 20 x 32 metres

3 Stor Gul Kanin, 2011
OpenART Biennale, Örebro (SE)
Concrete, metal, wood, takspån
13 x 16 x 16 metres

4-6 Dushi, 2009
Gallerie West, The Hague (NL)
Assorted textile, site-specific
video installation
Various sizes

How do size and scale matter to your projects?

Everything. To change your perspective you need to scale up or downsize your subject, so it can be viewed as if you've really lain down or flown above it.

In my case, I make it most of the time many times bigger, also of the materials I use. They are often meant for construction needs. They have this human to handle size, therefore they bond so much with us because they look and feel familiar.

To what extent do your creations interact with the public, space and the environment?

By looking at the images concerning space and the environment when I work in public space, the interaction already starts as we make plans for the building of an artwork. My subjects and locations always relate. Most of the time I do site visits up front so I know the places, history and feel, which are all grounds for my ideas. If you work in public space you need to know how you can alter it. You need to know the strong and interesting points of a site which you can change in the long or short term.

While we're working on site me and my crew are also in constant contact with the audience. We meet and talk at the sculpture's site. The work starts there, but it's not only about the end result but also the way towards it. People see the work grow and get attached as they are curious about what this work will become, and how it's going to evolve. It's also about communication and getting in contact with your audience and the public space. Often we become friends with those who come back often to see the process.

What is it like creating and building sculptures that are many times bigger than you?

I am always curious about whether we can manage to do it again. It'll make a big surprise if it all works out like planned.

Every time at the beginning of each project I model most of the works before I actually build, so I already saw how my sculptures would likely look as well as the interesting parts. Having visited the site before and knowing the environment, the history, lines of the landscape and approaches of the audience, I know I can begin my work and bring my concept in. It's also about building together and make things happen. It makes you feel proud as a crew and that you have overcome things again!

How do you exaggerate things while making them believable?

I look for the right location and make them simple to understand. I think it might rather be the way we work and the materials we use that made for the exaggeration.

The variety of materials employed is another highlight of your creations. How do meanings transform as they become part of the larger object?

I search all the time for new material and apply methods to create the skin. It depends on the work every time, on the concept and the location. It all goes hand in hand.

When the material is applied to build, it doesn't stand on his own any more but serves a bigger cause which is the object. It's all about making close-ups, zooming in and out again. It's also about seeing and understanding and getting surprised by these materials as they become something else.

As for *Slow Slugs* (2012) installed in Angers, France, I used 40,000 plastic bags which I wanted to make a work already for a long time. With the slow slugs the bags generate in the wind a sort of movement and glimmer like they are wet.

Viewers are often allowed to get close to your sculptures. How does it help to reinforce the experience?

People start to look and taking pictures. Inviting them to enter a work, walk around and feel is a different approach to the senses.

Where did the temporary installations go after the event?

Sometimes they come back to my studio, sometimes we find a place to put them and expose them again, sometimes we need to destroy them. It's part of the work. You make temporary works to change public space and then again to show the public space as it was before. Sometimes we can re-use the project and the piece will be constructed again somewhere else.

What are you planning on producing next?

A big dead fly in Mexico.

(The Dead Fly has been realised as a site-specific inflatable in Nov 2012, to reinterpret the Day of the Dead, a typical Mexican celebration to honour the deceased.)

072

Radford Wallis is a London-based multidisciplinary visual communications agency committed to approach design with fresh, distinctive and quirky ideas for functions ranging from branding and marketing campaigns through to real-life installations, websites and signage design. For the immense grade-A office space at 80 Victoria Street, the largest part of Land Securities' Cardinal Place office development in London, Radford Wallis was approached to display the potential division of the floor plate to let. Their solution was a larger-than-life stationery combo, fixed on the floor, awaiting prospective tenants to examine and be amused.

INTERVIEW
WITH

RADFORD WALLS

What was the project about?

80 Victoria Street is the largest part of Land Securities' Cardinal Place office development in London SW1. One of the enormous floors of 80 Victoria Street was to be split into four smaller sections and let to separate mid-sized companies, by building four partition walls. Letting agents who would show prospective tenants around the vast empty floor space required something to clearly demonstrate the future division of the floor. Our clients were looking for a practical solution that simply and clearly communicated the division of space, even within such a large floor plate. It was the need to communicate clearly in surroundings of such scale that led to the idea of building giant 3D objects.

Why are physical dividers and flat signage systems not enough for the project?

The floor plate size was just over 50,000 square feet or just over 4,600 square metres. An empty floor plate of that scale needed something which would stand out and grab people's attention. There might well have been a creative solution with physical dividers or a flat signage system that could have achieved this too, but the giant stationery objects created a memorable and very powerful physical presence as soon as you entered the space.

80 Victoria Street, Division of Space, 2007
London (UK)
Mdf timber, mild steel, polyurethane resin
machining slabs, cellulose spray paint, vinyl
graphics
1 (Scissors) 4 x 2.5 x 1.5;
2 (Highlighter pen) 4 x 1.5 x 2.5;
3 (Tape measure) 3 x 3 x 1.5;
4 (Masking tape) 3 x 3 x 0.75 metres
Production: Main Titles

It seems that Radford Wallis' graphic solutions incorporate physical objects from time to time. How does it facilitate communication?

For us, it's about finding the right idea for the job. We also work in 2D and in digital media, so if the project is going to benefit from a 3D idea, we'll pitch it!

As for our 80 Victoria Street project, the physical giant objects communicated the idea more immediately and in a much more simple way than a 2D solution ever could have. It was a mixture of the viewers' surprise at experiencing the giant installations on entering the space and the question that the objects immediately posed in the minds of those who viewed them. It achieved a simple mixture of impact and message, without the need for explanation. The scale of these everyday and familiar objects also had the added benefit of appearing fun, whilst impressing with the bold commitment to reproduce them beautifully. The finished pieces would not have looked out of place in a gallery. By contrast a 2D interpretation of the same idea could have been reproduced at the same scale for impact but it would not have had anywhere near the same impact in terms of the bold impression that was made and left in the minds of those who experienced them first hand, especially when you consider that people were there to view the space and not giant objects installed to make a point.

Why did you want to render stationery items? How did they relate to the prospective tenants of the office space?

Four everyday items that could be used to mark out or divide space were chosen: a tape measure, roll of masking tape, pair of scissors and a pink highlighter pen. Obviously the stationery items have a relationship with the office environment that would be created on the floor plate as a witty link.

Viewers were there to see potential office space for a company's staff to operate from. The everyday office items reproduced as giant objects made a link in the minds of those who came to view the space by 'humanising' an empty architectural space that had been created for the use of office staff but as an empty floor plate, in itself would not have communicated or implied the office worker. By using the everyday familiar desk objects, the link or connection of the floor plate as a space to be used by people, was made in a non direct and quirky way. Each of the stationery items was chosen for their everyday ability to draw a line or potentially divide space.

What kind of impact have size and scale added to the promotion in particular?

By scaling up the familiar everyday office objects to a size befitting of their surroundings, the twist in scale echoed the huge proportions of the floor space available. The scale enabled them to be seen together as a set from a distance from any point on the floor plate.

To what extent would you say the items have interacted with the environment and space?

Their scale was certainly intended to make them work in relation to one another within such a generous space, so as visitors walked around the space, all the giant objects would be visible from any point. The divisional lines that were created by the giant objects, cut across the floor plate to visually break up the space. The lines gave a sense of scale within the overall space by creating imaginary walls that each divided the floor, whilst connecting graphically with each other.

What is key to turning everyday objects into a spectacle?

The key to this is the detail. It has to look exactly as you imagine the actual items to be. The model makers did an amazing job ensuring that everything was recreated perfectly, not just visually but also with the materials used.

How well do you think large installations prompt public participation in commercial projects nowadays?

Large scale installations make art very accessible and break down boundaries, encouraging people to interact with them. The larger the piece, the more it seems to be owned by everyone.

Where did the sculptures go after the campaign?

Some of them were featured in a D&AD exhibition and after that we're not sure. Maybe they're in a stationery cupboard. All the giant objects were created true to the original stationery objects, with no building specific branding, only that of the stationery manufacturer appeared. This meant that in theory, they could be used in any building to delineate space in a similar way, if required.

What are you planning on or hoping to produce next?

As designers, the projects we work on are determined by the clients we work with. We aim to try and make them as relevant and engaging as we can. It's about making the most of every opportunity.

Drawing inspiration from as well in defiance of everyday life and urban surroundings, British artist, Luke Egan, a.k.a Filthy Luker's diverse and outlandish urban installations awake the desire for fun and fantasy in city-dwellers. Motivated by the love of interventionist art and the endless possibilities within medium, self-taught Filthy Luker diversifies his expressions through a range of agencies, including mouldable foams, found objects and most remarkably inflatables that could pop up anywhere in the world. As well as his personal work which he calls "Art Attacks", he co-runs Designs in Air, where he creates inflatable sculptures and public art projects with Pete Hamilton, a.k.a. Pedro Estrellas, since 1996.

INTERVIEW
WITH

FILTHY LUKER

You describe your street-level installation art as "Art Attacks". What kind of attacks have you attempted to bring to the streets/people on the earth?

I see my Art Attacks as a kind of cartoon assault on mundane reality, like Wile E. Coyote with his ACME pranks on The Road Runner.

I also call them Art Attacks as the installations are only temporary and need to make a big impact in a short time. Rigging the installation is usually a team effort and has to be quick and well planned so the whole process of getting the sculpture out of the workshop and up becomes a kind of surreal military operation.

How did you get into the realm of oversize installation art? How long have you been in your practice?

As an artist the interest has developed from studying plant-life and tiny organisms as inspiration for inflatable shapes and the idea of creating a giant world has evolved to include scaling up everyday objects too. It is easy to make large inflatables, so seems rude not to.

I have been making inflatables for around 17 years now, often working with designer, Pete Hamilton. We are completely self-taught and neither of us did a degree in art. There isn't a course you can do in making inflatables anyway and there is also no affordable 3D design software that has an 'inflate' button.

1 Russian Anti-Gravity Pencil, 2011
St. Petersberg (RU)
Ripstop nylon, centrifugal fan
1 x 5 metres

2 Eyeball, 2010
Geneva (SW), London (UK), Quito (EC)
Printed PVC
2 metres in diametre

3a Octopied Building, 2008
Maubeuge (FR)
Ripstop nylon, centrifugal fan
1.5 x 10 metres (each)
Collaboration with Pedro Estrellas

3b Nightmare on Hill Street, 2005
Totterdown, Bristol (UK)
Ripstop nylon, centrifugal fan
1 x 5 metres each

3c Cottage Industry, 2010
Tyrol (IT)
Ripstop nylon, centrifugal fan
1.5 x 10 metres each
Collaboration with Pedro Estrellas

3d Quito Kraken, 2010
Quito (EC)
Ripstop nylon, centrifugal fan
1.5 x 10 metres each
Collaboration with Pedro Estrellas

3e High Diving Octopus, 2011
Geneva (SW)
Ripstop nylon, centrifugal fan
1.5 x 10 metres each
Collaboration with Pedro Estrellas

4 Down the Plughole, 2011
Royal West of England Academy, Bristol (UK)
Ripstop, 4oz nylon, bendy MDF, plywood
(Plug & hole) 3 x 0.6, (chain) 30 metres

5 Bananadrama, 2008
Bristol (UK)
Foam, 4oz nylon, latex balloons
4 x 8 metres
Photo: Ross James

How do size and scale matter to your projects?

It's funny how a mundane object can be so striking when rendered as a huge object, but I don't think shear scale makes a piece interesting — there needs to be some relation to its environment.

There is a perfect size where a piece is big enough to make impact but not so big it's unmanageable. Because of the nature of the medium and the type of installations we do need to consider the weather, especially the wind and the method of installation. We often work to tight budgets, personally funded or commissioned, so we generally want to make the design efficient in materials and build time, how we will transport it and put it up.

Some artists take on materials to convey meanings. Does it apply to your projects too? How do they add to the viewers' experience of your projects?

We are fairly restricted to certain non-porous materials that can be inflated, so I try to stick to making things that look good with the look of these materials. I think the synthetic qualities of nylon emphasise the out-of-place occurrence of a disproportionate object. We almost never paint or print on our cloth to try and hide this like many other inflatable manufacturers, but instead rely on good panel work to create form and texture. For me there is also an irony in that I am often making art about nature using non-natural materials.

Did you choose the exhibition sites? To what extent would you say your art interact with its environment, location and the public?

Many of the sites I have chosen, though some sites I have been asked to work with. I have tried to work site specifically and also make things that can be used and installed in many ways. I have a big bag of oversized objects to choose from and it's interesting how an object redefines itself through its environment.

What was it like building objects that were many times your size?

It's a little different than you might think with inflatables, as a huge piece can just fold up on the table and you're only ever sewing up a little part of it at one time. When designing something on a computer it could be any size, so sometimes when it's time to blow things up it can be a bit like, "OOoops! I accidentally hit the XXL button!"

Everyday life objects have been integral to your sculptures. What kind of impact does magnified reality have on the viewers?

I think that scale has an impact on all of our lives as children in a world that's been built for big people, but then when playing with miniature toys scale gets flipped on its head again and we imagine blades of grass as huge trees, rocks as mountains, puddles as oceans. Encountering giant objects can take us back there I think. Being faced with out of proportion objects forces us to observe the object in a new way as well reassess the world around us. Perhaps it puts things into a more realistic and humbling perspective in that we are just tiny beings in a huge universe.

Some of your work play on illusions to excite — we could imagine a monstrous octopus struggling in a building just by seeing its arms sticking out from the windows. How did it enrich your creations and viewers' experience?

I love this concept and try and use it as much as possible for many reasons: The sculpture requires an interaction with the environment to be completed and it activates the spectators' imagination as they must fill in the gaps — they must collude with the artists' concept to get the picture. Last but not least it uses fewer materials and takes up a bigger space — with just two painted beach balls my sculpture can be as big as a tree!

Where do your sculptures go respectively after the events?

Into a bag marked "toys".

What are you planning on producing next?

Working with a guy called Jnr. Hacksaw and a mixed media team we call 'Under Pressure Art'. We are developing ideas that allow people to remotely manipulate and interact with the sculptures using custom coded software, animatronics, sensors and artificial intelligence.

ANCIENNE MAISON PAIN
FONDÉE EN 1859

Born in Chicago and currently based in New York City, Kurt Perschke is an artist who works in sculpture, video and collage besides his most acclaimed travelling public art project, the *RedBall Project*. Having stopped over in Abu Dhabi, Taipei, Perth, England, Barcelona, St. Louis, Portland, Sydney, Arizona, Chicago and Toronto, the giant ball opens a doorway to imagination as it uses its stiff red body to challenge space. Although it has been Perschke's intention to catalyse new encounters within the everyday, the deeper significance of the project lies in the way each city responds to that invitation to engage and, over time, what the developing story reveals about our individual selves and cultural imagination.

INTERVIEW
WITH

KURT PERSCHKE

How did you come up with the RedBall project? What was the notion behind?

The piece came directly out of my working with an urban site for a commission. I had been offered an opportunity to come up with an idea for one of three sites in St. Louis through the Arts in Transit program. I kept coming back to this ugly area underneath an overpass with a bit of gravel on the ground. It had clearly been offered up because it was one of those leftover spots in a city, but I was drawn to the way the concrete bridge merged into the earth and the space it created. *RedBall* came out of my thinking about that space, and how to show what I was seeing. After many false starts I drew this huge red sphere under the bridge, and laughed out loud. I felt like that was it.

RedBall looks as simple as a red ball although it occasionally tends to challenge space and height. Why did you think such a ball is up for the job? What is its charm about?

RedBall challenges space all the time! Simplicity is something to strive for because it enables so much participation in the viewer, however it's rarely simple to achieve. *RedBall*'s directness, its magnetic presence, its willingness to occupy unusual spaces, to be humorous, these are all ways of inviting an audience in. Ultimately the work is not about the ball at all, its about the energy being created around that space out of an act of imagination.

RedBall Project
Barcelona (ES), Abu Dhabi (AE), London (UK),
Korea, Belgium, Sydney (AU), St. Louis (US),
Arizona (US), Norwich (UK), Chicago (US),
Portland (US), Toronto (CA), Taiwan
Ferrari precontraint fabric
Max. 4.5 metres in diametre

Since when travelling the world became part of *RedBall*'s agenda? What has the journey added to the ball?

The project travelled from the very start. After its launch in St. Louis, I was frustrated by the constraints of not being able to move it through the city. So I took it to Barcelona and worked with a curator and artist friends who helped out to create it there. It was all illegal street installations except the MACBA site, and it was in some ways that was the real beginning of *RedBall*. The sense of motion it has in a performance — of moving through a city — is echoed in how it moves around the world. This journey and its travels are very much part of how the piece is experienced at an imaginative level. Of course standing in front of it that moves to the backdrop and the experience is direct.

How do size and scale matter in this project?

Scale is a tool. Size is just what a tape measure reads, but scale is experienced. With *RedBall* the scale is changing all the time, you only really understand this when you've been able to see it move through a few sites in a city, then this sensation of it getting larger or smaller begins to be realised on a bodily level. Often people are surprised by this. They are not used to the experience that — like time — scale is relative to our perception.

Did you pick the exhibition sites? How are the locations and architectures relevant to your idea?

I travel to each city far in advance to find the sites. The selection of sites is the creation of the artwork. The ball is only an object. The performance is the joining of site+audience to it. As a process I go to each city, a year in advance usually, and literally walk and bike the streets looking. I carry a camera, a sketchbook, and a laser meter and go exploring a city, getting very lost over and over. What I am looking for is a collection of sites that together might make a great project. Some sites offer architectural excitement or history, others are at a nexus of pedestrian energy. I am always hunting for great sun and the chance for surprise. Really seeing is an active state. For the serious *RedBall* site hunters out there, check out a book by Christopher Alexander et al. called *A Pattern Language* (1977); it's a codex of the psychology of our architectural environment.

The RedBall Project allows the public to get close to the ball and have fun with it however they like. How is it important for the project and the public?

In making a public work I am very conscious of the history of sculpture in public places, its origins in monuments, and how that leads — for better or worse — into a perception of what public art should be today. RedBall is riffing on all that static mass in the permanent hierarchy, and instead exploring the living space of a city. The urban environment is overbuilt and full of possibilities, and the project is about seeing and playing with the sculptural spaces of a city. The humour and charisma of the piece allow its access to the city and invite others into its story. I think it's essential for public work to do more than be 'outdoors' — it needs to live in the pubic imagination. Simply being placed in public space does not make a work public in the communal sense. Scale, tactility, physical presence — these are all tools of sculpture and here they are used as an invitation. Creating a sense of play is serious business.

You've received quite a number of suggestions from the public about where to put the ball in the participating cities. Care to share some fascinating ones?

I've gotten invites from school children, architecture students, fan — you name it. And not just in cities where it's happening but all over the world. This week some invitations came in from a Gymnasium in Croatia! And others from Moscow, Switzerland, Brazil, Milan, etc. The project invites this openness, though I can't unfortunately go to all of these places. For me, all the ideas that flow in are part of the essence of the work — people participating in the imagination of the work. So for me one idea isn't better than another, but more that every idea is someone joining into the act of participatory imagination.

You brought up an interesting point about turning art into a star in the interview conducted by UICA. Can you expand on the idea?

In that talk I was speaking to students, and I think there is a lot of corrosive ideas out there pushing the goal of artist stardom, and it gets in the way of what developing artists really need to be doing, which is focusing on their work, their practice, and their peers as a support network. The cruellest thing 'art star' goals do is silently shrink the realms of possibility for artists. I work all over the world, but my career has no relationship to that star track. There are many, many ways to be a working artist in the world.

Is there any particular place you want to take and display RedBall? Where would it go if people/cities stop inviting RedBall over for a visit?

Well, I hope the invites don't stop because there are so many places still to go! I have ideas, and sometimes the project has its own ideas. I would love to go back to the Middle East and the Gulf. I learned a lot in Abu Dhabi so I would be excited for that. Istanbul is a favourite possible site. South America would be new, and there are some interested folks in Brazil. Asia is overflowing with great cities, I've just done a visit to Hong Kong for *RedBall*, and Kyoto has always been a dream. The project responds to invitations...I don't push it, it has its own flow.

What are you planning on producing next?

RedBall has grown and I'm working on how to let it keep doing its thing while I make time for other ideas I want to fund and put out in the world.

Gerry Judah (b.1951) is a British artist of Iraqi descent. Taking imaginary landscapes, architectural fantasies and futuristic car drawings as placebo since he moved to London with his family at the age of ten, Judah studied fine art and sculpture in college and university before he began to design settings for television, museums and theatres, and work on large sculptures for public arenas outside the rarefied gallery space. Before returning to his fine art roots to explore the effects of war and environmental catastrophes recently, Judah has been the architect behind the spectacular sculptures at the annual Goodwood Festival of Speed, that celebrates history and speed.

INTERVIEW
WITH

GERRY JUDAH

What is Goodwood Festival of Speed about? How did your collaboration start?

The Goodwood Festival of Speed is probably the most important annual event in the world which celebrates motor sport and cars. The collaboration started with Lord March when he was a photographer way back in the 1980's where I used to build scenery for him. In 1997, he approached me to design and build a giant triumphal arch to hang a Ferrari F1 car, and it took off from there. Since then, each year he has asked me to come up with concepts for a different motor car company who were celebrating their achievements in motor sport, which also coincided with their centenaries and other anniversaries.

What was the thought that immediately popped into your head when you were approached for the project?

Because the Festival of Speed is such a major event for motor sport and for cars generally, each company sponsoring the Central Display see it as a terrific platform for them to celebrate their history and their ethos. So I don't design brands. I start from the spirit of the company. After lengthy discussions with them as well as Lord March, I come up with ideas which I feel fit not just the company's spirit but also the grandeur of the event itself. Sometimes it takes a long time to come up with an idea but often it takes a moment — and there it is!

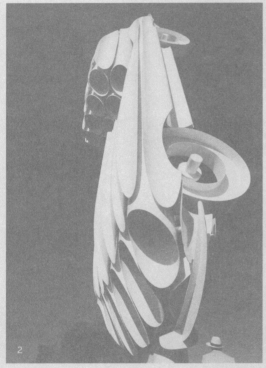

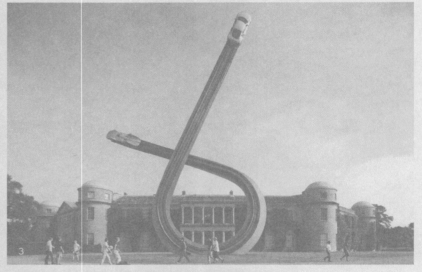

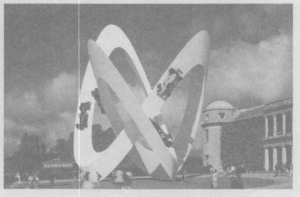

1 Alfa Romeo Central Display, 2010
Goodwood Festival of Speed,
West Sussex (UK)
Steel
19 metres in height

2 Jaguar E-Type Central Display,
2011
Goodwood Festival of Speed,
West Sussex (UK)
Steel
28 metres in height

3 Audi Central Display, 2009
Goodwood Festival of Speed,
West Sussex (UK)
Steel
34 metres in height

4 Lotus Central Display, 2012
Goodwood Festival of Speed,
West Sussex (UK)
Steel
29 metres in height

Special credits for all projects:
Engineering: Capita Symonds
Fabrication & installation:
Littlehampton Welding
Photo: David Barbour

After collaborating with more than ten car manufacturers for over a decade, what have you identified between them, which then appeared in your sculptures?

I know that most cars are the same; they have four wheels and take you from A to B, but each company has its own identity and my job is to bring it out in the expression of the sculpture. Rolls-Royce's endeavours are different to Mercedes-Benz, which is different to Lotus. For example with Lotus I felt the innovation of the monocoque that Colin Chapman developed in the manufacture of his cars was quite a good story to tell, so the sculpture itself was a giant monocoque, without any internal structure — 98% of it was air, which was brilliant in engineering terms. The brief with all of these sculptures is that they all have to be as large as possible, because of the event — innovative in terms of the design and engineering — and have an element of danger to them, so that when you stand near, it frightens and overwhelms you. In a sense that's what these cars do, so they need to be displayed in an exciting and original way.

How do you visualise 'speed' with quiet and static cars? What inspired the dramatic effects in your works?

It can be difficult to make a car look like it's moving at a hundred and whatever miles per hour in a still setting, but I think the sculpture is not about showing them in the moment of speed, but rather the moment of "animated suspension", like the feeling you get when you enter a temple. So the sculpture has to have an element of spirituality and power. After all, the visitors attending the Festival of Speed are making a sort of pilgrimage to see their motor sport heroes and icons.

Why did you want to move your works outside galleries and display in more public arenas? Was it when you began to work on large sculptures?

Art galleries and museums are great on one level because, again like a temple, they offer a hallow space which also helps you concentrate your belief in the art. Once inside, you're a captive audience. Of course the work has to befit the space. I tend to prefer work which reaches a wider public, hence my involvement with film, theatre, opera, ballet and so forth. So in a way, these are events of sculpture on a public arena, where people can walk or drive past them, whether it's in a high street, a park or an estate. It's a shared experience on a wider level. That's probably why architecture appeals to me a great deal. We also now live in the world of the 'wow-factor' and its global accessibility. With the Olympics, it wasn't just the athletes or the sports that one was looking at; it was the event, the stadia, the paraphernalia — the big statement — and size fits that requirement.

Does your creative process involve a lot of engineering or architectural work?

Initially, I have a general idea, a sense of what it is I want to do. Then I draw a lot, make sketch models using cardboard and any material I can lay my hands on. I work a lot with engineers which means a great deal of negotiation between fantasy and reality, art versus pragmatism. So to make things work, one needs to engage engineering values right from the beginning. Computers also play a very important part, so we employ programmes like AutoCad to help us along the way.

Global conflicts in nature, politics and races is another focus of your work. What in these subjects fascincates you most?

They're all connected. The car sculptures and the war paintings have a lot in common because they have to do with history in their own way. Art often celebrates history but it also holds a mirror to it. Also I suppose the elements in my work are about power, the power of speed and endeavour, and the power of hate and destruction. It's also the will to succeed, to win, to be the victor at any cost.

Where did your Goodwood sculptures go after the events?

Often they get destroyed because they are designed only for the event so the engineering and fabrication are made on that basis. The car company who sponsors the sculpture often wish they could re-site it outside their headquarters but that requires a very different approach, which impacts on the budget and on planning issues, so we let it be about the event. Having said that, the Alpha Romeo sculpture is at the Cass Sculpture Foundation without cars and the E-Type Jaguar sculpture is in storage awaiting confirmation for a suitable site outside the Jaguar headquarters.

What are you planning on doing next?

I've recently returned from India where I was taken by Christian Aid to look at their projects to combat climate change. I'm working on a series of installations relating to my experiences there, as I was also born and grew up in India for my first ten years. There are a lot of personal connections as well as environmental ones, so I think the work will be quite radical. I'm also developing some potential sculptures for a site in New Zealand, and for next year's Goodwood Festival of Speed.

122

Founded in 2004 by Koichi Suzuno and Shinya Kamuro, TORAFU ARCHITECTS employs a working approach based on architectural thinking. Stimulating thoughts and desire to explore in the combination of practicality, imagination and simple materials, works by the firm encompass interior designs for shops and exhibition space, as well as product and experience design which appeal to users of all ages. The "Word Park" inside *Y150 Nissan Pavilion* (2009) and *Gulliver Table* (2011) in Tokyo Midtown DESIGN TOUCH park were characteristic of TORAFU's astonishing approach to engage, featuring respectively air as a material and a table that seems to grow in proportion as it inclines towards the end.

INTERVIEW
WITH

TORAFU ARCHITECTS

Both founders of TORAFU were trained as architects. What kind of architectural logic have you taken to reinforce your concepts?

We give the products some grounds or conditions and come up with concepts to solve problems, just the same as the way we think about architecture.

What were *Nissan Y150* and *Midtown DESIGN TOUCH* about?

The Nissan Y150 Dream Front pavilion was designed as part of the EXPO Y150 initiative commemorating the 150th anniversary of the opening of the port of Yokohama. Located in a warehouse on the Shinko Pier, the Nissan Motors PR project spanned two areas focusing on children and the environment.

Tokyo Midtown DESIGN TOUCH thinks of design as all things that make up culture, such as interior accessory or graphics, products, music and cuisine. Based on this view and their advocacy of "enjoying design with all five senses", they introduce events suggesting that our daily life is being enriched by these factors. In order to differentiate from TOKYO DESIGNERS WEEK and DESIGNTIDE TOKYO which are held at the same time, this event has workshop for parents and children.

1 Y150 NIssan Pavilion, 2009
Port of Yokohama, Yokohama (JP)
Air, inflatables, paper
(Balloons) 4.5 - 10 metres in diametre,
(Floor area) 2196m²
Production: TBWA, HAKUHODO
Planning: HAKUHODO
Construction: MURAYAMA
Photo: Daici Ano, Alessio Guarino

2 Gulliver Table, 2011
Tokyo Midtown DESIGN TOUCH Park,
Tokyo (JP)
(Table top) Lauan plywood,
(Table legs) SPF lumber
2.4 x 50 metres
Structural design: Ohno JAPAN
Production: Ishimaru
Photo: Fuminari Yoshitsugu, TORAFU
ARCHITECTS

132

The idea of using air as a material recurs in TORAFU's recent projects. Why air? How did the idea guide your design for Nissan Y150?

The air was the material for the balloon that became 3D when they inflated, giving them the aspect of solidity when virtual images were projected onto the round surfaces of the 0.5mm thin membranes. Natural light coming down from the sky passed through layers of transparent and opaque membranes; casting and distorting shadows of visitors moving between the spheres and giving the whole space its tone and atmosphere in a hazy mix of projected shapes and shapeless forms. We sought to give the pavilion an ever-changing, enchanted atmosphere with its many reflected images and to eliminate the tributary itself. The relationship between the ground and figures were represented here by the open space and spheres respectively. All these responded and reflected Nissan's vision for a future with clean air.

Giant bubbles were running all over the space in "Word Park". What kind of experience did you intend to bring to the visitors and Nissan Y150 Dream Front Pavilion?

"Word Park" is a large exhibition space. These 16 giant bubbles ranging from 4.5m to 10m in diametre gave the surrounding space its physicality, inviting visitors to playfully navigate through it. Visitors could also leave messages on a leaf-shaped note and put it in the balloon which would then whirl and dance around like blue leaves inside the balls as air was introduced. We did this to entertain and trigger visitors' behaviour. Children enjoyed this pavilion more than we expected.

How was space relevant to the settings in EXPO Y150?

We used the potential of this big space as much as possible. The spheres touched at certain points, supporting each other and creating a feeling of tension. To see these way of construction was really exciting.

Why did you want to build a table for Midtown DESIGN TOUCH? What were your considerations for the Gulliver Table's design?

At that time, space for workshop was required, so we designed a space that people can visit anytime and stay in several way. Regarding the details, we teamed up with structural engineer to work out the thickness and balance of the legs so that it would look like a real table.

To what extent do you think size and space help catalyse communication today?

We think that communication happens regardless of the size of the space, it depends on the relationships between people.

Your projects have constantly been a place of wonder for both adults and children. What would you say is crucial to your success?

For *Gulliver Table*, We designed the margin that people can stay in several ways at different height. This kind of margin is really important because both adults and children can find the place where they like.

Where did the balloons and *Gulliver Table* go after the event?

The balloons were folded up until it became really compact and the manufacturer took them back. We don't know what happened afterwards but maybe they were recycled.

As for *Gulliver Table*, we donated all the materials to Ishinomaki Laboratory. The *Gulliver Table* was designed to be recycled from the beginning. The wood were screwed together and easy to scrap.

Ishinomaki Laboratory is 'a place of creating something new' for the community, established by designers and others in Ishinomaki, a city devastated by the March 11 Tsunami. The collaboration with Ishinomaki Laboratory allowed sky-deck to be manufactured by the people of Ishinomaki, making this product commercially available.

What are you planning on producing next?

We are always trying to derive each project's feature and find what we can do only in the project. At the same time, we would like to create something that allows people to accept various things.

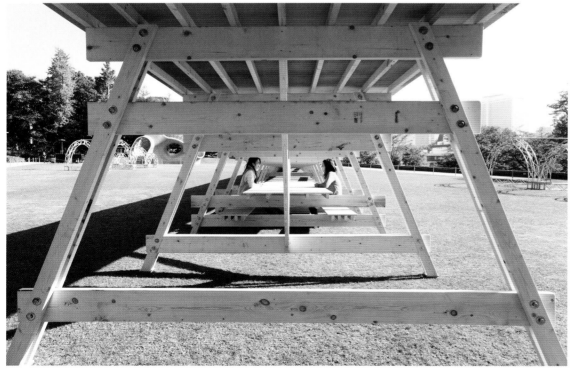

Based in Ontario, Canada, Dan Bergeron, aka fauxreel, takes street interventions to question the notions of public space. By embedding human faces in urban landscapes, he reclaims spaces for the excluded or ignored. In *Gaspesia: Les portraits en Papier*, four larger-than-life portraits revived the tragic closure of Gaspesia in 1999, leaving the city of Chandler an urban wasteland rife with widespread social and environmental problems. Through these drawings of men who previously worked at the pulp and paper mill, the project marked the physical structures of the mill and laid claim to its history and continuing impact on the city before its demolition.

INTERVIEW WITH

DAN BERGERON

What was *Gaspesia: Les Portraits en Papier* produced for?

Gaspesia: Les Portraits en Papier was produced for the 2011 Rencontres Internationales de la Photographie en Gaspésie. I was commissioned by the festival to create an installation related to the city of Chandler, Quebec where the pulp and paper mill was located.

Where did the idea come from? Why did you want to tell the story of Gaspesia and its former staff?

The idea to document the former workers of Gaspesia pulp and paper mill stemmed from my interest in connecting people to the spaces or communities that they live and work in. I had already completed a previous project documenting workers and installing their images in a closed down brick factory in Toronto in 2009, so I saw the opportunity to document the former workers of Papiers Gaspésia as an extension of this earlier project. I think that it is important to remember and to celebrate the work that people do, especially when their work is so closely tied to the social and economic identity of a town, like the way the pulp and paper mill is tied to Chandler, Quebec. To remember the contributions of the workers is especially important in this day and age as we are witnessing a dramatic shift in how and where we work due to the technological revolution we are currently experiencing.

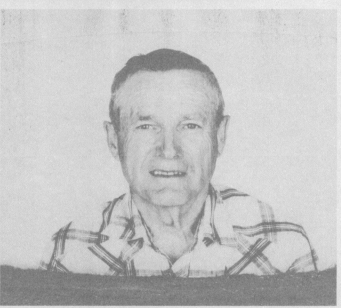

Gaspesia: Les Portraits en Papier, 2011
Rencontres Internationales de la
Photographie en Gaspésie, Quebec (CA)
20 lb oversize paper, wallpaper adhesive
11 x 9.2 metres

Why did you choose to make portraits on paper in an open area?

I often create portraits on paper and adhere the images to architectural sites. The practice is known as wheatpasting and for this project it seemed to fit perfectly as the subjects were former workers at a pulp and paper mill. Another nice thing about using paper is that it wears away with the weather, making the work ephemeral and allowing it to age just as people do.

Who was your intended audience and why?

As Gaspésie has a number of tourists during the summer, I was obviously interested in creating images for them to look at during their stay in Chandler and the surrounding area. That being said, the most important audience for me for this project were the townspeople of Chandler and the subjects themselves. I wanted the subjects to come out of the project feeling really great about themselves, and for the townspeople of Chandler to recognise these workers and their contributions as well as remember the history of labour that the city was originally founded on.

How do size and scale matter to your project?

The large scale of the work was essential so that the installations could be seen from far away. As the pulp and paper mill was closed down and fenced off, viewers were not able to get closer than 100 feet from the mill. In addition, because the buildings were so large, it's important to make the installations suit the size of the architecture.

What was it like creating and completing such enormous images? What made them powerfully evocative, even for the ones who know little about Gaspesia?

This is not the first time that I have completed installations at this size, so it didn't faze me to work at this scale. In terms of the strength of the portraits, I try very hard to make my subjects comfortable and confident about themselves. I asked them to think about waking up in the morning and looking in the mirror. When you are all alone at this time of the day you can be your true self. As such, I find that when I captured the subjects with this direction, they struck poses that are confident, relaxed and honest. Theses emotions would then translate to the viewer, allowing the viewer to make a strong connection to the subject.

To what extent did your creations interact with the public, space and the environment?

For this project the installations interacted more with the environment and architecture of the mill rather than the public. As the mill is closed to the public and fenced off it wasn't really an option to make the work interactive on that personal level.

Faces have been a recurring theme in your projects, why? What can a face tell?

A large part of my practice involves documenting people and installing their images in the community that they live or work in. I have chosen to do this because people create communities and the built environment around us and it's important to recognise one another and the contributions that we have made for the greater good. And although I sometimes shoot full-body portraits, more often than not I shoot facial portraits because the face is the main vessel for human communication.

Where did the portraits go after the event?

The portraits have remained on the mill and will until they naturally wear away due to the weather. It's very ephemeral this way and I liken it to layers of skin peeling away from the human body.

What are you planning on producing next?

I'm currently working on a project for the City of Toronto in which I'm documenting a group of Chinese seniors who practise Tai Chi in Grange Park behind the Art Gallery of Ontario. The images of the seniors will be transferred to tiles so that the installations will be permanent and they will be installed in Toronto's Chinatown neighbourhood.

151

GALLERY

These 28 artist profiles, with over 40 recent and significant projects of the age, are the essence of what make for the most incredible real-life encounters for both adults and kids. Featured units include artists, designers and international agencies with varied expertise ranging from car manufacturing to product design.

STUART MURDOCH

Pimm's Deckchair, 2012
Bournemouth Beach, Dorset (UK)
Mild steel, printed PVC mesh
5.7 x 9.7 x 8.5 metres
Production: (frame) Metalcraft Cornwall
Photo: Solent News

Meet the world's heaviest deckchair, standing at 8.5-metre high and weighing over 5.5 tonnes on Bournemouth beach in Dorset, England. Commissioned by English fruit cups brand, Pimm's, the chair was unfolded with a frame of mild steel hollow section beams and air permeable printed PVC mesh to welcome the advent of British summer time. The work of Stuart Murdoch, the sculptor behind the project, mainly commissioned for events and campaigns, has been standing out in the juxtaposition of contemporary culture, art and engineering. Much of his influences comes from his vast experience as a special effects supervisor in the fields of advertising and TV.

DAVID WEEKS STUDIO

Giant Cubebot, 2012
Salone del Mobile, Milan (IT)
Coated polyurethane foam, metal
1.77 x 3.05 metres
Special credits: Quinze & Milan, Areaware

Robots are always the best friend for boys and men who feel young in their hearts of heart. Designed by David Weeks, who also has a knack for innovative furniture, lighting and household product design, *Cubebot* is an unorthodox take on the toy robot. Inspired by Japanese Shinto Kumi-ki puzzles. At 20 times its original size, giant

Giant Cubebot joins ancient Japanese traditions with contemporary toy culture at MOST salone during Salone del Mobile 2012. With his roots in Athens, Georgia, he now resides with his wife, Georgianna Stout, partner of design studio 2x4, and his children in Brooklyn (New York, US).

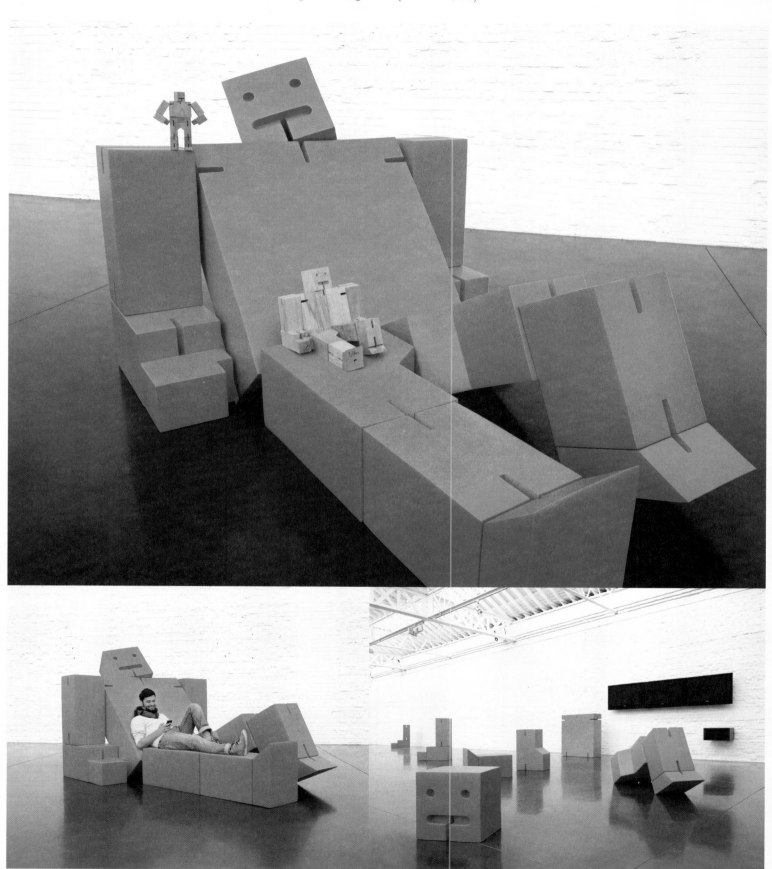

NEARLY NORMAL STUDIO

Big Butt Project, 2010
London (UK)
Colour paper, old newspaper, steel wool
0.12 x 0.4 metres on average
Special credits: Monique

Directed by Jaime Kiss and Elias Torres and produced by Nearly Normal, *Big Butt Project* was initiated to draw Londoners' attention to the phenomenon of habitual littering with their diverse reactions recorded on tape. By dramatising the size of cigarette butts and placing them conspicuously on Central London walkways, the project made the problem visible to all, whether they were responsible for it or not. Nearly Normal is a London-based boutique creative studio led by Brazilian duo, Jaime Kiss and Saulo Jamariqueli, who specialise in projects ranging from branding to stop-motion films. Elias Torres is an experienced Brazilian creative director at VCCP.

CHRIS WHITEBURCH, AUSTIN NELSEN

The Purge, 2012
Texas (US)
Scrap wood, debris
4.88 x 9.75 x 3.05 metres
Special credits: Vladimir Mejia, Nick Griffin,
Erich Rodriguez, Nick Miller

The Purge was fundamentally a New Year's resolution gone wrong. As a sequel to art collective Ink Tank's 2011 January show which depicted a family's response to the coming of doomsday in form of one final New Year's Eve bash, the 2012 version pictured a house's reaction to the impending doom, expelling not only the obstructive or destructive but also its main structures. *The Purge* was co-developed by Chris Whiteburch, who works primarily in installations and sculptures, and Austin Nelsen, in sculpture, photography and graphic arts. Whiteburch and Nelson are both members of artist-run non-profit, Co-Lab Projects.

ZARKO BASESKI

Zarko Baseski (b.1957) is a sculptor of Macedonian descent. His realistic sculptures have sought to quest after human's psychological changes through life and unique features of Macedonian art. Introduced at Baseski's latest exhibition in 2010, *Ordinary Man* and *Philip II Macedonian* (2010), together with *Self-portrait* (2010), a life-size model of the artist himself, recognised man as the symbol of ongoing existential struggle. While dimension has not been key in the concept, the unusual size of *Ordinary Man* expresses a desire to rise above mediocrity and transcend one's self.

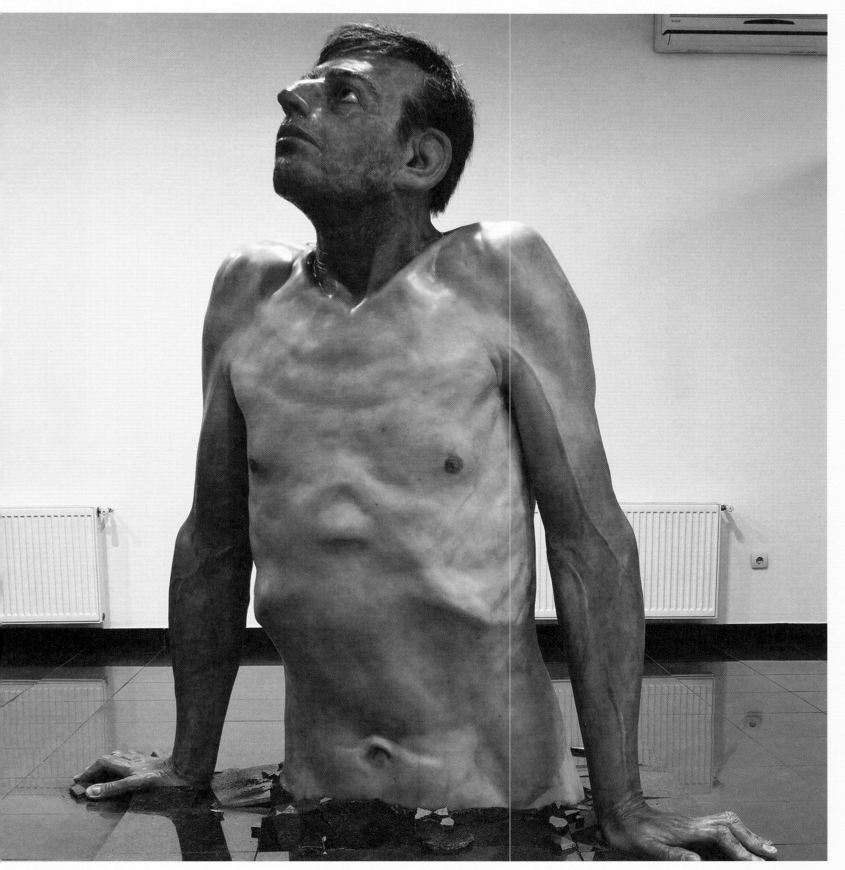

Ordinary Man, 2010
Culture and Information Centre, Skopje (MK)
Polyester resin, fibreglass, silicone, hair
2.2 x 2.25 x 0.75 metres

STUDIO JOB

Entirely covered in 24K white gold mosaic and glisten, *Silver Ware* is an eight-piece collection designed for luxury mosaic brand, Bisazza's *Limited Edition* collection first exhibited at Milan Design Week 2007. As a perfect fusion between utilitarian design and art, the set features Cake Platter, Silver spoon, Tea Tray, Dish Cover, Chandelier, Candle Holder, Tea Pot and Basket on permanent display at Bisazza's headquarter in Italy. Studio Job is a Dutch-Belgian duo Job Smeets and Nynke Tynagel, based in Antwerp and the Netherlands. Since 2000, the collective has set themselves to redefine decorative arts for the contemporary age with primarily one-off work through traditional crafts.

Silver Ware, 2007-8
Milan (IT), New York (US)
24K white gold mosaic
(Basket) 1 x 1.75 x 1.75: (Candle holder w/candle)
1.92 x 1.66 X 1.4; (Cake platter) 0.76 x 2 x 2;
(Teapot) 1.86 X 2 x 1.14;
(Dish cover) 1.17 x 1.89 x 1.89 metres
Photo: Jean-Baptiste Mondino (left), Paolo Veclani

NENDO

Totalling 4000 pieces, the mass-produced non-woven fabric hats were the antithesis of Akio Hirata's carefully handmade hats exhibited at Hirata No Boshi, as the internationally-known Japanese milliner's first major retrospective of 70 years of work. Floating and streaming through the gallery's geometric space like ghosts or shells of the real hats on display, the installation softly invited visitors to wander around Hirata's hats, as a way to physically experience the creative freedom that underlay Hirata's work. Gracefully executed, the project was created by design firm nendo who promises to realise designs with small surprises. nendo was founded in Tokyo in 2002, currently headed by Oki Sato (b.Canada, 1977).

Hirata No Boshi, 2011
SPIRAL, Tokyo (JP)
Non-woven fabric hats (4,000pcs)
(Gallery space) 160m² x 12.6m

EVANTA MOTOR CO.

Vintage cars charm mechanic fans and antique collectors for its aesthetics and technical achievements at various points of time, but the reproduction of Aston Martin DBR1 in 2012 means more than this. Born out of a passion for delicate British sports cars, Evanta hand-manufactured a life-size DBR1 "AirFix" model not only to commemo-rate its victor in the 1959 Le Mans, but also the legend of its drivers, Carroll Shelby and Roy Salvadori, and chief engineer, Ted Cutting, whom all sadly passed away in different points of 2012. Evanta Motor Company is a privately owned family business based in Hertfordshire, the U.K..

Aston Martin DBR1 "AirFix", 2012
Hertfordshire (UK)
Fibreglass / kevlar shell / handcrafted
aluminium panels over superleggera framework, new or fully reconditioned parts, etc.
3.4 x 6.35 metres
Photo: Richard Pardon Photography

LIESBETH BUSSCHE

Concrete balls as black pearls, chain link as bracelet onto which charms can be put, pearl necklace waiting to light up the street when the sun goes down... now with Liesbeth Bussche's *Urban Jewellery*, cities can certainly be personified as a 'she'. Brought up in a small Belgian village, Bussche has developed a love for cities when she went to school in Antwerp and Brussels. Often site-specifically designed with care and installed unauthorised, Bussche's urban interventions are subtle and simple, and yet a spectacle for everyday life. Bussche now operates her own art practice in Amsterdam, the Netherlands.

Urban Jewellery, 2009-12
Cagnes-sur-Mer (FR), Arnhem (NL),
San Francisco, California (US), Taiwan
Various sizes
Special credits: (Suzy's charms)
The town of Cagnes-sur-Mer

MICHAEL JOHANSSON

Michael Johansson deals with ordinary objects in a way far from the ordinary. Driven by the agenda to densify the world, his work features objects morphed into precisely stacked rectangular shapes in relation to space, where original intentions transformed into catalysts of new meanings, as in *The Move Overseas*. Bringing objects a step back in the line of production is another current in the Swedish artist's work. Presenting gears and tools cast into life-size assembly kits, *TOYS'R'US*, *Some Assembly Required — Hard Hat Diving* and *Assorted Garden Assembly* made a commentary on today's ways of living: a display of function without functionality.

171

BEN LONG

Like 3D sketch renderings brought to life, Ben Long's *Scaffolding Sculptures* first appeared in 2004 as temporary artworks inspired by his experiences working on building sites as a teenager. Reusing the same metal tubes and scaffolding systems for his collection, his work at once asserts the value of a disciplined working practice, the hard graft of manual employment and significance of the construction industry in urban development. Born in Lancaster, UK, 1978, Ben Long is a contemporary visual artist operating predominantly within the public realm. Much of his work features focuses on aspects of British working culture.

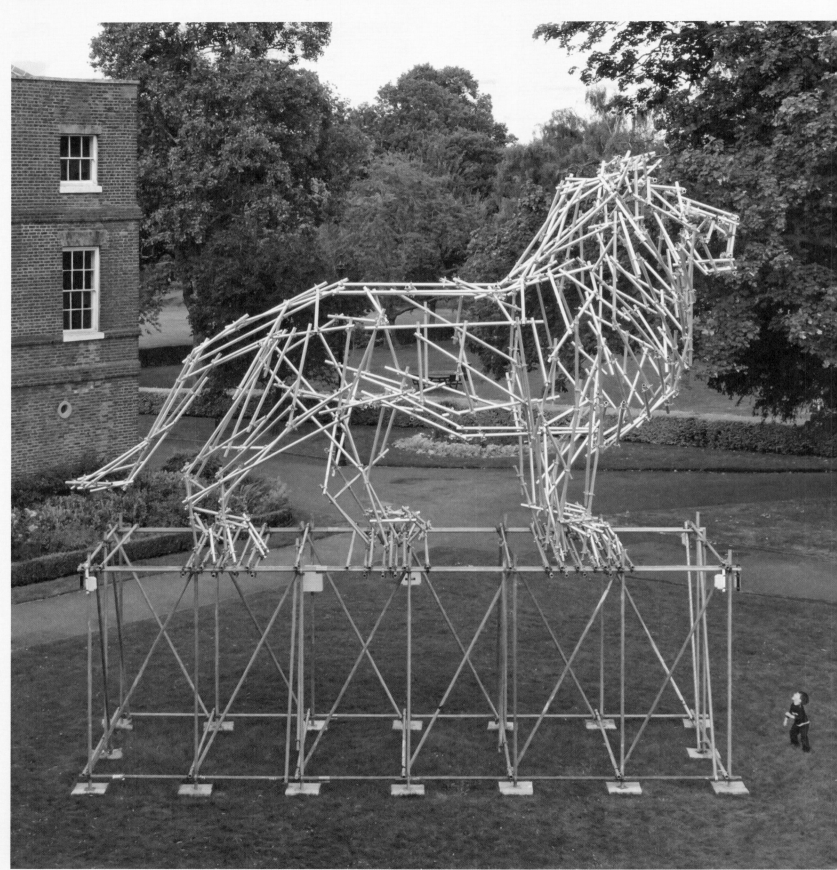

Scaffolding Sculptures, 2009-12
(Lion) Bruce Castle Museum, (Horse) The
Economist Plaza, London (UK)
Scaffolding systems
(Lion) 10.13 x 3.41 x 9.06,
(Horse) 4.72 x 3.41 x 8.09 metres
Photo: (Lion close-up) Stephen White

CHRISTOPHER WEED

Red Paperclips, 2011
Colorado Springs, Colorado (US)
Steel tubes with epoxy primer
and urethane finish
7.32 x 1.08 x 9.76 metres

Positioned at the Plaza of the Rockies, overlooking the Pioneers Museum, a Colorado Springs landmark, the interlocking *Red Paperclips* explored forms and function at a precarious yet well-balanced state. The project was a first-prize winner at 2009 Art on the Streets. Born in 1963, in Philadelphia, Pennsylvania, Christopher Weed now resides in Colorado Springs and uses primarily luminous materials, size and bright colours to get viewers transported with whimsy. He has obtained a BFA from the University of Maryland and completed over 20 public art installations since 1999.

MEHMET ALI UYSAL

SKIN II, 2010
Festival Cinq Saisons, Liège (BE)
Wood, earth, metal
15 x 10 x 6 metres
Photo: Zoé Baraton
Special credits: Pi Artworks

Mehmet Ali Uysal (b.1976) is a Turkish artist who has been seeking to recover the meaning of architectural spaces through the language of art. Taking elements from everyday life, Uysal materialises space which, for him, records and internalises human experience. *Skin II* was one of his attempts to draw the public's attention to the ordinary ground of a park during Festival Cinq Saisons, with a giant clothespin gripping the ground as if it was a flap of skin. Uysal is currently represented by Pi Artworks, one of the leading contemporary art galleries in Istanbul.

JEAN JULLIEN

Built into the apex of Tour Bretagne, the tallest building in Nantes, France, Le Nid ('The Nest' in English) is not only the home of an enormous white bird, but doubles as a bar and livable art space by Le Voyage à Nantes. Measuring roughly 40 metres long, the half-stork half-heron guides visitors to explore the city's scenic view while offering its neck and eggs as tables and seats. French graphic designer Jean Jullien from Nantes but currently based in London was the man behind the project's concept, art direction and design. His illustrations and graphic solutions are known for a 'handwork' quality, charged with popular culture from his childhood.

Le Nid, 2012
Nantes (FR)
Rubber, plastic
40m
Production: Métalobil
Special credits: Le Voyage à Nantes,
Urban Makers, Niwouinwouin

THE PROPOSAL

Too Fat To Fail is a living tribute to the gigantism of our times, referencing Manuel Uribe from Mexico, the fattest human alive. Having been on display at THE PROPOSAL in Zurich, the naked giant also aspires to squeeze into New York's Grand Central Station one day. *Too Fat To Fail* is created by artist and curator, Jeremie Maret (b.1982) who co-founded THE PROPOSAL, with Lenny Staples and Christian Weber in 2011. Exhibition guests were as well invited to enjoy a special bed-and-breakfast service to live in the artistic ambience inside the gallery space.

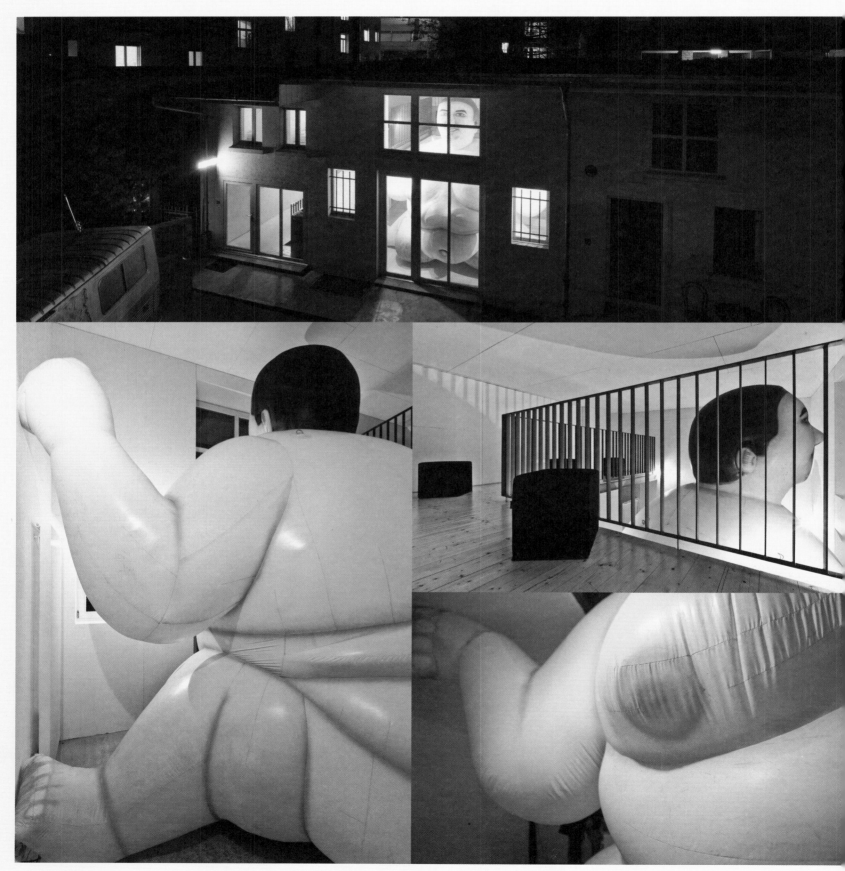

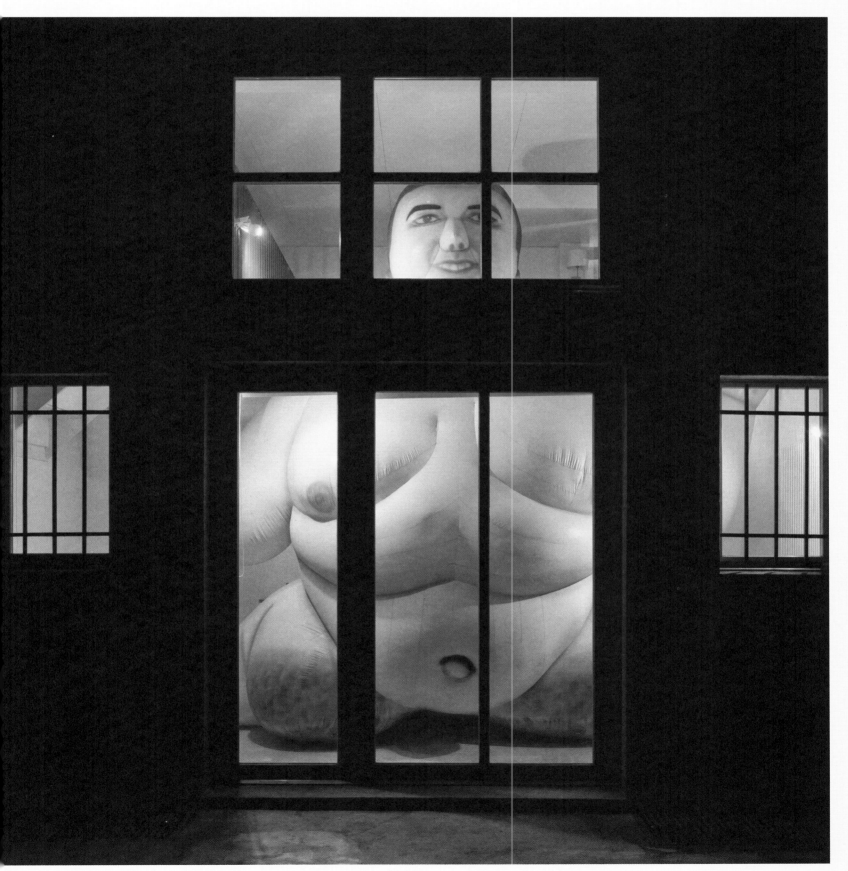

181

SAGMEISTER & WALSH

Renamed as Sagmeister & Walsh after Stefan Sagmeister added Jessica Walsh as a partner in 2012, the New York design studio creates identities, commercials, films, books and objects literally for all. *Everybody always thinks they are right* was produced during the Sagmeister Inc.-era. for Six Cities Design Festival initiated by the Scottish government. A total of six white angry monkeys, each held one word of the statement, were individually displayed on an eminent location inside Glasgow, Aberdeen, Edinburgh, Inverness, Dundee and Stirling. The public was encouraged to complete their experience by visiting all six Scottish cities or through the media.

Everybody always thinks
they are right
, 2007
Six Cities Design Festival, Scotland (UK)
Inflatables
Each 10 metres in height
Design & typography: Stefan Sagmeister,
Matthias Ernstberger
Illustration: Monika Aichele
Production: Joel Mangrum, Sportogo Inc.
Coordination: Ailsa MacKenzie,
Stephen Roe, Stuart Gurden
Photo: (Inverness) John Paul,
(Other cities) Mark Hamilton

LA BOLLEUR

Started off as a restaurant, and later a mini golf club, La Bolleur works between Amsterdam and Eindhoven, the Netherlands, with amusing prints and installation projects visible in theatres and design festivals locally and across cities like Milan, Berlin, London and Shanghai. Having twisted and tied balloon animals at various occasions, the Dutch studio brought forward the fun of balloon sculptures to the city centre of Eindhoven during the summer of 2010. Each balloon dog were fabricated from gigantic tubular balloons made of colourful kite fabrics, ranging from 6 to 25 metres long.

Balloon Animals, 2010
Eindhoven (NL)
Kite fabrics, electric fans
6 - 25 metres in length

URS FISCHER

Untitled (Lamp/Bear) is a stark union of a canary yellow teddy and a generic desk lamp that define a young boy's room. Appearing lovingly hand-sewed and soft as it leans forward, the sculpture is in fact a 35,000-pound bronze cast replica of a real teddy from childhood. The lamp is operative with an acrylic light bulb that had lit Seagram Building's plaza for five months and now permanently the shore of Montauk. Currently based in New York, Swiss-born artist Urs Fischer began his career in Switzerland where he studied photography at the Schule fur Gestaltung, Zurich. *Untitled (Lamp/ Bear)* has been recently sold through Christie's for USD6.8 million.

Untitled (Lamp/Bear), 2005-6
Edition 1, Seagram Plaza, New York (US);
Edition 2, Home of Amalia Dayan and
Adam Lindemann, Montauk, New York (US)
Cast bronze, epoxy primer, urethane paint,
acrylic polyurethane topcoat, acrylic glass,
gas discharge lamp, stainless-steel framework
7 x 6.5 x 7.5 metres
Special credits: Galerie Eva Presenhuber, Zurich

Photo: Cary Whittier

Photo: Dean Kaufman

189

CHOI JEONG HWA

Korean artist Choi Jeong Hwa's work satirises 'speed' and 'expansion' as the twin falsehoods of Korea's modernisation. Motorised to inflate and deflate, the ceaseless movements of his balloon lotuses constitute a metaphor for life cycles and at the same time the beauty and emptiness inherent in momentary life. Currently based in Seoul, Choi (b.1961) draws inspiration from popular or day-to-day items for his artistic work. While a heavy use of plastic makes for a commentary on the ubiquitous mass-produced products, he also works with media, such as videos and light.

1

ARAM BARTHOLL

German artist Aram Bartholl (b.1972) uses forms to create an interplay between internet, culture and reality. His works ask not only what man does with the media, but what media do with man. Rendered to be a simple 20 px graphic icon on computer screen, the virtual pin that Google Maps use to locate a place is also designed to appear physical with a simulated shadow, especially in aerial mode. Cast out of wood and wires, *Map* physically marks the spots that Google Maps assume to be each location's centre, and questions the relation of digital space to everyday life and city space as bytes transform into grams.

Map, 2006–10
Taipei (TW), Berlin (DE), Szczecin (PO)
Wood, wire, screws, glue, nails
6 x 3.5 x 0.35 metres

MICHEL DE BROIN

Measuring 7.5 metres in diameter, *La Maîtresse de la Tour Eiffel* was the largest glitter ball ever made by Michel de Broin. Poised 50 metres above the ground of Paris, the mirror ball recreated the sensation of the sky before light snowed the city, with five light projectors during Nuit Blanche, an annual arts festival which starts at six in the evening and ends before sunrise. Adopting a critical and playful attitude towards common objects and concepts, de Broin engages the public in the rethink of everyday matters through public art. De Broin currently settles in Montreal, Canada after living in Berlin, Paris and London.

La Maîtresse de la Tour Eiffel, 2009
Nuit Blanche, Paris (FR)
Metal frame, mirrors (1000pcs),
light projectors, crane
7.5 metres in diametre

MONSTRUM

Playhead, 2010
Copenhagen (DK)
Plywood, steel, paint
8 x 3 x 2.5 metres

Featuring an interior like a tortuous brain, prism-shaped eyes as light inlets, two hands and a swing, *Playhead* was a hybrid of a climbing frame and a slideway designed for one of the five art playgrounds constructed by the City of Copenhagen in hands with Peter Land. As well as playground structure, the head referenced artists, like Hi-eronymus Bosch, Pieter Brueghel and surrealists who had brought fabulous work to this world. Founded by Ole Nielsen and Christian Jensen in 2003, MONSTRUM approaches playground structures that emphasise visual design as much as safety, as a reflection of our world that captivates both adults and children at once.

MOTHER LONDON

London Ink, 2009
London (UK)
Polystyrene
(Swimmer) 10.67; (Girl) 5.49 metres in length
Production: Asylum
Tattoo design: Louis Malloy

If you wonder what the giant girl is doing in the photo booth, or to where the swimmer is crawling, walk around and you will find the answer on their waist and shoulder, with tattoos revealing the airtime and date for a new TV show, London Ink. British elements, such as chips and a "glorious pigeon", were added to the classic Japanese carp and war eagle tattoo designs to display at London Victoria station and near Tower Bridge. Mother is the UK's largest independent advertising agency founded in 1996, with offices also in New York and Buenos Aires. Its philosophy is "To make great work, have fun and make money. Always in that order."

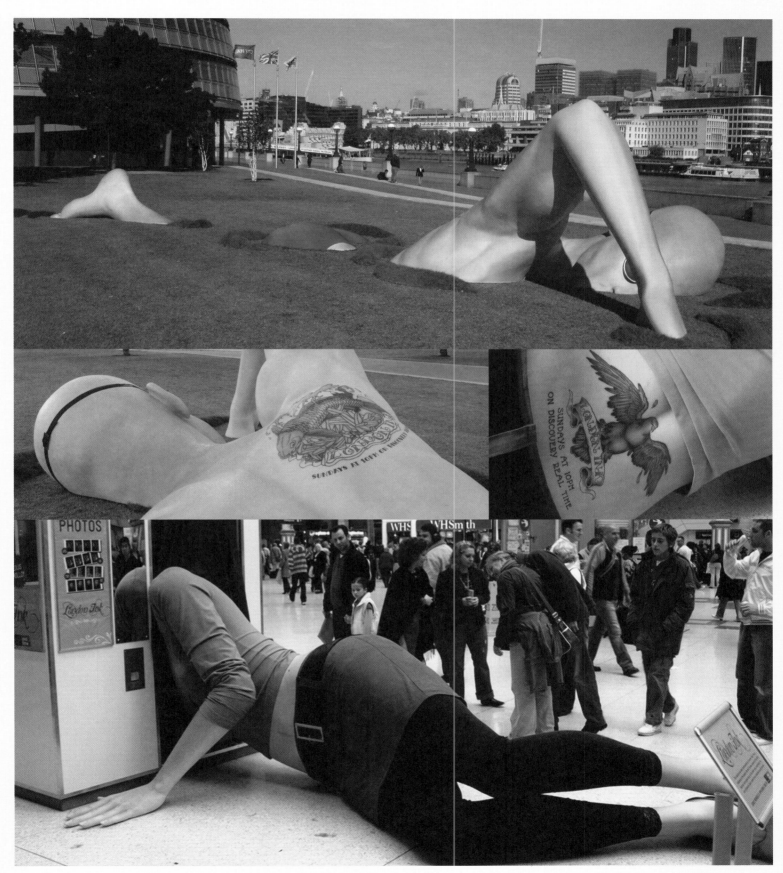

199

SEWARD JOHNSON

One of the most influential artists in contemporary American art scene, Seward Johnson has created more than 250 life-size cast bronze figures exhibited in major cities across the world. Besides his realistic *Man-On-The-Street* collection which debuted in the 1980s, *ICONS* is yet another masterpiece series that seeks to rekindle the attitude and optimism of the time that celebrities and iconic figures represent. *Forever Marilyn*, capturing Marilyn Monroe's skirt-blowing key scene in *The Seven Year Itch* (1955), is the latest from Johnson, currently standing in Palm Springs, California. The collection also features *Unconditional Surrender* (2005) in Florida and *The Awakening* (1980) in Maryland, US.

OLIVER VOSS WERBEAGENTUR

For ten days, Alster Lake in Hamburg has been turned into the world's largest tub with the presence of *Bathing Beauty*. Rising four metres above the water with her knees up before public eyes, the blond stretched 10 metres long in the water to demonstrate the art of bathing as the spokeswoman for British beauty brand, Soap & Glory. Art and advertising agency, Oliver Voss had creatively directed the project in hands with Till Monshausen. The agency is a team of ten, headed by Voss who founded the company in 2010 to offer creative solutions in both realms of art and advertising.

Bathing Beauty, 2011
Alster Lake, Hamburg (DE)
Fibreglass, plastic, aluminium, cosmetics
4 x 10 metres

Creative direction: Oliver Voss,
Till Monshausen
Art direction: Florian Zwinge
Graphic design: Peter Ardelt
Production: Mhoch4 GmbH & Co. KG,
Cornelius Rönz, Hanna Duin, Daniel Behrend
PR agency: lauffeuer Kommunikation GmbH

ADEL ABDESSEMED

Currently based in Paris, Algerian-born Adel Abdessemed (b.1971) attended the École des Beaux-Arts in Algeria before moving to Lyon, France in 1994 due to political unrest, where he continued his fine arts education. Pulling freely from personal, social, historical and political sources as well as arts, Abdessemed employs a broad range of media to put up his statement about the sinister side of the world. Forces of violence and destruction are visible in *Telle mère tel fils*, where aeroplanes were extended into plait-like structure, and *Habibi*, where a giant skeleton, propelled by jet-engine, hovered before viewers' eyes.

1

1 Habibi, 2003–6
Berlin (DE), Geneva (SW), Paris (FR)
Resin, fibreglass, polystyrene,
airplane engine turbine
3.5 x 21 metres
Collection of the MAMCO, Geneva
Photo: Thomas Bruas

2 Telle mère tel fils, 2008
New York (US), Paris (FR)
Airplanes, felt, aluminium, metal
4 x 27 x 5 metres
Collection of Budi Tek
Photo: Cathy Carver

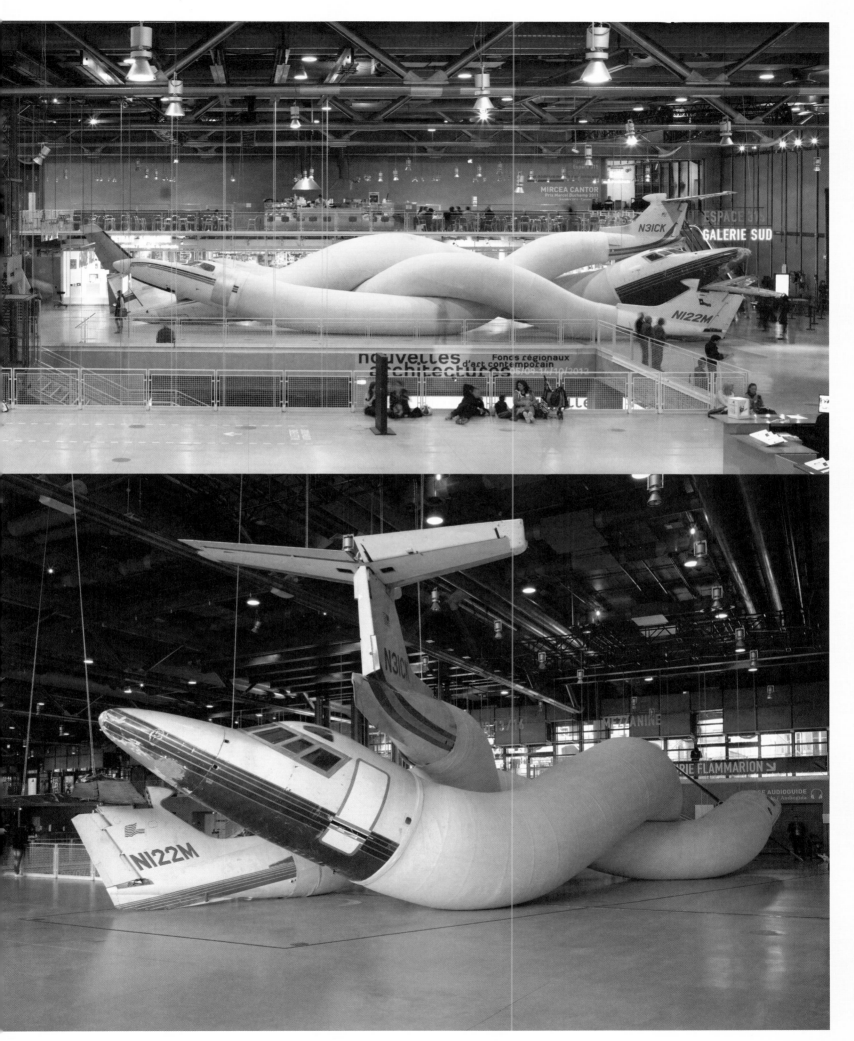

ATTACK INTERVENÇÕES URBANAS

PETS made a call for recycling PET bottles along the bank of Tiete River, São Paulo. Tied up in a roll to visually revive the most important river in the metropolitan area, the 20 gigantic inflatable soda bottles were destined to be transformed into inflatable schoolbags after the event. Originally a visual artist specialising in painting, Edu-

ardo Srur gradually discovered his interest in new media, spanning photography, sculpture, video performance, installation and urban intervention art. Through his art creation, Srur takes on urban and environmental landscapes to raise question against social system in a critical and humorous way.

PETS, 2008
Tietê River, São Paulo (BR)
Vinyl fabric, floating platform, PET soda
bottles, modules and galvanised iron,
steel cables, anchoring system, wiring and
electrical system, fluorescent lamps
10 x 3.2 metres each

GORDON YOUNG, WHY NOT ASSOCIATES

Commissioned as part of the extensive regeneration programme at Blackpool, a popular holiday destination for the Brits, *Comedy Carpet* celebrates comedy with over 160,000 granite letters embedded into concrete, where visitors could recapture classic jokes, songs and catchphrases by over 1,000 comedians and comedy writers and watch shows upon the project's completion. The project was cre-ated by artist Gordon Young, and designed in hands with Why Not Associates. Young is a visual artist who focuses on reinventing language and word forms for the public domain. Why Not Associates is a celebrated graphic design agency specialising in advertising, publishing, branding and public art.

Comedy Carpet, 2011
Blackpool (UK)
Concrete, granite letters (160,000pcs)
(Floor area) 2,200m²
Typography: Why Not Associates
Photo: Angela Catlin, Jonathan Farman,
Rocco Redondo, Why Not Associates

INDEX

OVERS!ZE
THE MEGA ART & INSTALLATIONS

First published and distributed by
viction:workshop ltd.

Unit C, 7/F, Seabright Plaza, 9-23 Shell Street, North Point, Hong Kong
Url: www.victionary.com   Email: we@victionary.com
www.facebook.com/victionworkshop
www.twitter.com/victionary_
www.weibo.com/victionary

Edited and produced by viction:ary

Concepts & art direction by Victor Cheung
Book design by viction:workshop ltd.
Cover image by Studio Florentijn Hofman

ISBN 978-988-19439-8-9
Printed and bound in China

Acknowledgements

We would like to thank all the designers and companies who have involved in the production of this
book. This project would not have been accomplished without their significant contribution to the
compilation of this book. We would also like to express our gratitude to all the producers for their
invaluable opinions and assistance throughout this entire project. The successful completion also owes
a great deal to many professionals in the creative industry who have given us precious insights and
comments. And to the many others whose names are not credited but have made specific input in this
book, we thank you for your continuous support the whole time.

Future Editions

If you wish to participate in viction:ary's future projects and publications, please send your website or
portfolio to submit@victionary.com